TOWARD TOTAL POETRY

ADRIANO SPATOLA

Toward Total Poetry

*Translated from the Italian
by Brendan W. Hennessey & Guy Bennett
with an Afterword by Guy Bennett*

OTIS BOOKS / SEISMICITY EDITIONS
*The Graduate Writing program
Otis College of Art and Design*
LOS ANGELES ● 2008

The translators would like to thank Polly Geller for her assistance in the preparation of this book, and Paul Vangelisti for his careful reading of the translation.

© Bianca Maria & Ricardo Spatola for the estate of Adriano Spatola
Published originally as *Verso La Poesia Totale* (Italian) (Torino: Paravia, 1978)
English Translation ©2008, Brendan W. Hennessey & Guy Bennett
Afterword ©2008, Guy Bennett

Book design and typesetting: Rebecca Chamlee

ISBN-13: 978-0-9796177-2-0
ISBN-10: 0-9796177-2-3

OTIS BOOKS / SEISMICITY EDITIONS
The Graduate Writing program
Otis College of Art and Design
9045 Lincoln Boulevard
Los Angeles, CA 90045

www.otis.edu
www.gw.otis.edu
seismicity@otis.edu

Table of Contents

Author's Note

Confronted with the vital "disorder" characterizing the variety of positions that currently comprise the panorama of new research, scholars may find a phenomenological approach not only useful, but necessary prior to any attempt at systemization. When we speak of "positions" we mean "poetics," according to Luciano Anceschi's definition, which seems consequent with respect to *Toward Total Poetry*: "every poetics claims to be the only poetics, yet poetics are infinite in number."* Naturally, this is not the place to debate the validity of such a definition; it is so totally open that, were we to push things a bit, it could very well neglect significant aspects of the poetics/poetry relationship. Nor are we particularly concerned with outlining the function of the poetics/aesthetics binomial that Anceschi brings into play on quite another level, and that is far less amenable to certain forms of absolute negation or dissolution. The fact is that a method demonstrates its function only when it functions, and not otherwise. Here Anceschi's phenomenological discourse works perfectly, for as soon as one considers these poetics from a standpoint that takes both existent and preexistent material into account, one is able to affirm that what is "about to happen" has the same right to exist as what has already happened. Apparently, no sooner are they identified (and this is what we have sought to do), than these poetics seem to slip

---

* Luciano Anceschi, *Progetto di una sistematica dell'arte* ["Project for A Systematics of Art"] (Milan: Mursia, 1962).

[Regarding the translation of titles: When Spatola translated titles in languages other than Italian into Italian, we likewise translated them into English; where possible, we indicated the American edition of the works in question. In the event that the work never appeared in English, we retained the original language title, and gave a translation of it in brackets, as above.
– *The translators*]

away; they are "dogmatic, normative, idealizing," and are no longer recognizable in the dimension that they themselves developed.

It goes without saying that such a mode of self-repudiation has a positive side, through which events that have "happened" take on the (even technical) sense of re-elaboration. With respect to the idea of poetics put forth by Anceschi, total poetry is consumed at a speed that can no longer be measured: it depends for many of its aspects on evident attempts to avoid the very problem of poetics itself (often not taken as such, but rather as a "dependent" mechanism). Suffice it to say that the material focused on in *Toward Total Poetry* is constructed so as to trace a number of already present structures. The list of these structures is available in this book and it is clear that to repeat it here would be to suggest that the book originates from a previously constituted network of references. Such a proposition is absurd: the distinction that Anceschi draws between "horizon of comprehension" and "pragmatic horizon" is used here as a means to demonstrate its validity, and in this note I can do little more than assert that only the acceptance of poetics in action has allowed me to write a book *on* poetry rather than a book *of* poetry.

— A.S.

1. From "Category" to "Continuity"

The experimental attitude constitutes one of the fundamental
points of reference for situating poetry, and originates from a
presupposition that the permanence of an imaginative surplus on
the part of the operator and any harm inflicted upon the user are
illegitimate. The objective is to establish a controllable equivalence
between the level of transmission and the level of reception. We
are dealing with an appeal for interdependence (horizontal and
vertical) and this interdependence is no longer structured simply
as an attempt to synthesize user and operator, as in a "going
towards," which finds its justification in its method, exhausts
itself, then continues within itself, according to Husserl's model
of the "surprising" Galilean idea. It is a hypothesis that, "notwith-
standing verification, remains a hypothesis, and will always
remain so; the verification (the only one possible) is a series of
infinite verifications."* The resulting interlanguage is apparently
centrifugal, dispersed in poetry. It is not the superimposition of a
linguistic system given to reality, but an invention, in reality, of a
total/fundamental linguistic system capable of any type of communication. By and large, the hypothesis cannot be anterior to contact
with reality, nor can the interlanguage be obtained by way of an artificial schematization of the problem of a sociologically free (open)
imagination. The Surrealist type of centripetal hyperlanguage, for
example, demonstrates how the imagination can be consumed by
such a question. On the contrary, for Tzara and the Dadaists, the
problem was easily exhausted through the "anti-philosophy of
spontaneous acrobatics." In this way, the experimental attitude

---

* Edmund Husserl, *Crisis of European Sciences and Transcendental
 Phenomenology: An Introduction to Phenomenological Philosophy* (Evanston:
 Northwestern University Press, 1970).

leads us to make of the poetic text an object free from the notion
of style and its corresponding mental category (order, cataloguing).
The interlanguage of experimental poetry claims to present itself
to either the operator or user as a method of adventure, a system
of disorder and, since research is impossible without planning,
this resulting contradiction is "creative." We know that the need
for contact between researchers who work in the most diverse
fields of experimental culture (those that we can define as experimental media) appears as the symptom of a situation that seems
new from certain points of view, but from others seems linked
to the protohistory of the avant-garde. The very concept of "intermedia," recently introduced by Dick Higgins, is no longer simply
a technical definition, like "mixed media" for example; rather, it
produces a mental attitude for which every distinction between
the various cultural forms must disappear. Higgins maintains
that the idea of category must be replaced by the idea of continuity. Continuity is the only possible relationship between such
diverse artistic activities that thus blur into one another. The arts
of our century, according to Heissenbüttel as well, are characterized by the tendency to move toward zone-limits in which each
individual art form brushes against the borders of the others, often
encroaching upon their territory. Up until the first decade of this
century it was entirely normal to establish precisely the technical
and formal differences between a painting and a literary text or
a literary text and a musical work. During subsequent artistic
development, however, other stimuli intervened, making such
distinctions both difficult and superfluous. In the phonetic poetry
of Hugo Ball, Raoul Hausmann, and Kurt Schwitters, for example,
music and literature, not to mention the theatrical elements that
played an essential role in their public readings, are all perfectly
fused together. According to Heissenbüttel, the zone-limits "favor
mixture and produce new kinds of art," and we are thus presented
with a result that exceeds a simple sum of factors, one that presents
unpredictable characteristics with respect to initial data. Kandinsky
agreed that the various art forms exchange techniques and notions:
"It can be asserted that in music the line supplies the greatest
means of expression. It manifests itself here in time and space just

as it does in painting. How time and space are related to each other in the two forms of art is a question by itself which, with its distinctions, has led to an exaggerated scrupulousness and, thereby, the concepts of time-space or space-time have been differentiated far too much."[*]

Theater merges with sculpture, poetry becomes action, music turns into gesture and at the same time uses pictorial-type procedures in its notation: terms like "happening," "environment," "mixed media," and "assemblage" are indicative of this cultural situation. The music of John Cage is one notable example since it collects and unifies many of these concepts, and Michael Kirby is indeed right to speak of the profound influence of Cage's ideas on all the arts beginning in the 1950s. According to Kirby,[†] Cage integrated certain dominant aspects of the Futurist and Dadaist traditions into his work, and the integration is evident in both the "simultaneous conferences" (the superimposition of live voices on taped voices) and the proposal of a "simultaneous representation of unrelated events." But perhaps even more interesting are Cage's calls to abandon changes in aesthetics in favor of global changes related to daily life: "[We are now are able] (no matter where we live) to do music ourselves. I am speaking of nothing special, just an open ear and an open mind and the enjoyment of daily noises."[‡] Many of his other "theoretical" writings bear witness to the meaning of this attitude.[§] Above all it is a mental hypothesis that, given the vast range from music to joke, from anecdote to pure linguistic gesturality, from mycology to compositional technique, escapes the logic of any single cultural dimension, any single genre. Upon this unlimited, immeasurable keyboard, Cage types out his attempt to construct a series of questions about the relationship between past, present, and future in a world in which contemporaneity is already thought of as an absence of art, or how total art

---

[*] Wassily Kandinsky, *Point and Line to Plane*, trans. Howard Dearstyne and Hilla Rebay (New York: Dover, 1979). Against the point/line/plane triad, see the Lettrists' negative attitude.

[†] Michael Kirby, *Happening* (New York: Dutton, 1965).

[‡] John Cage, "Happy New Ears!" *A Year from Monday* (Middletown, CT: Wesleyan, 1963).

[§] John Cage, *Silence* (Middletown, CT: Wesleyan, 1961).

with in addition perhaps a few concessions to the mythology of the possible modernity of technological *trouvailles.* The resulting portrait depicts an individual of disconcerting vitality, a surprisingly anarchic *jongleur* capable of producing works of staggering precision.

The new arts thus reveal a critical condition of sensibility, customs, expressions, and thoughts, in a word, of all the social configurations that produce them. And this critical condition stems from a change in our vision of the world: we are becoming accustomed to consider objects with a different eye, to place them in a light foreign to them, utilizing relationships and connections that have yet to be pondered. "In this way of seeing, we act according to the stimulus of a thought imposed on us by the extant and insensate history of our existence during this century," writes Franz Mon. The arts present themselves as a response to the world, as a critical representation of this "hesitation." We are confronted with a thesis that directly empowers the social mandate of the experimental poet, and that makes the visual text coincide with its motivations in relation to a situation determined independently by the objective or "foreseeable" realization of the visual text itself, one that at times stands in opposition to that which Germano Celant has defined, in an analogous context as "object-apologia." If we thus consider intermedia as a general theory of the evolution from category to continuity, a theory applicable no doubt to the visual text, we can then assert that the contrast between mental freedom and the standardized application of the media creates a situation in which experimental poetry, once understood to be in contradiction with itself, can utilize that contradiction as a structure of communication. According to Jochen Gerz, "society is part of the museum, the reader cannot escape tautology." This assertion rings true because there is a reversal of real data (be it the museum, the book, or the poem as participating in society) at the moment in which the aesthetic value of the visual text is replaced by an evaluation of its potential as message, and often as *negative message.*

It has been noted that the overdeveloped world periodically sees the ideological/aesthetic foundations of cultural production as being in crisis. But if music, painting, poetry, and theater lost the support consolidated by their use, it would be naïve to claim that such terms are somehow no longer pronounceable solely because their physiognomy has been altered. On the other hand, even through the constant application of proven techniques that encompass the message, the socio-cultural relationship cannot remain unmodified by the subversion of preexistent models, regardless of whether this subversion has had a brief or long tenure, and whether it be fortuitous or planned. "In a period like the present of continuous and dynamic becoming," writes Gillo Dorfles, "there is no longer time for the static nature of reception and the reverential quality of contemplation. It is necessary to accumulate quickly and effectively (or perhaps quickly and ineffectively) the images that the world offers us, to somehow make them our own before they lose their sting and are lost into nothingness." And Franz Mon: "Ambiguity is concreteness. Everything that has been identified is already almost lost."

The fact is that a negative art has been proposed at regular intervals from the very beginning of the twentieth century, and that during this period words like "revolution" and "revolt" have been pronounced with the most inconsistent and opposite of meanings, but always to designate or provoke a state of crisis in the notion of art. Certainly the "permanent revolt" requested by Surrealist irrationalism has nothing in common with the "pieces of healthy young crude art" produced by the *revolution of content/revolution of form* binomial proclaimed by Mayakovsky. The negation is occasionally directed against local objectives and contingents, occasionally becomes absolute, provoking a chain reaction in which the point of departure – poetry, literature – finally disappears. Weighed down with commonplaces, reality likewise disappears in the name of various aesthetic alchemies. And yet the panorama of the historical avant-garde offers real surprises in the area of projects most "scandalously" conceived at the level of unfeasibility. And in this field, where programs blur and intertwine into works whose substance seems to escape objective definition, works impossible to place in one sector or another, but calculable only in terms of possibility/ impossibility no longer of a fixed cultural phenomenon, but by society itself in its own totality. It is a two-part global responsibility of the imagination. A dissolution – to what extent voluntary? – of art (of non-art) into the problematic of existence, of social rituality. If the conscience of this dissolution has traversed the historical avant-garde with its double valance of enthusiasm and desperation, only recently has a gust of mental lucidity fixed the needle of the compass on the irreversibility of the phenomenon. Then the discourse turns out to be unidirectional: art is objectively "non-art," objectively "commodity," objectively "useless." Russian Futurism's hope for a proletarian/collectivist art dissolves into planetary industrialization, the space-time of market laws, the pseudo-democratization brought about by television, literacy, advertising, the chain of montage, and by serial production. Inherent in this process of dissolution we have the constant presence in certain visual forms of poetry of an attempt at the "rehumanization" of signs, at the "revindication" of iconography. So, can poetry (art) survive? One might reply that the problem is no longer of any importance, that the response to such a situation is by now entrusted to individual decisions, biological impulses, choices that cannot be catalogued or explained according to the logic (or logics) of social systems, or at any rate of the very survival that we are discussing. But one might also reply, for example, that the loss or annulment of the ideological/aesthetic references in question has to do with the misunderstanding lived by Marinetti: "Though they seek synthetic forms of expression, philosophy, the physical sciences, politics, journalism, teaching, and business must still make use of syntax and punctuation. I myself am obligated to use them in order to explain my ideas to you." The lines that follow this assertion – "Futurism is founded on the complete renovation of human sensibility resulting from great scientific discoveries" – resemble in effect a compulsory demonstration, which is significant in that we are presented with the acceptance of an aesthetic dichotomy realized on the level of language in simply a-ideological terms. The passage from "language as instrument" to "the instrumentalization of language" is not far off, and immediately after, Marinetti could write (1913): "The cowardly, sedentary inhabitant of any provincial city can treat himself to the intoxication of danger by watching a big-game hunting movie."

The attack cannot be conducted by traditional means, so we must oppose the cultural apparatus with an unassailable, fleeting farce, with implications both tragic and mystical – but, Hugo Ball declared, "without a religious sensibility, monkey business is impossible." These "actions" are repeated against a background far vaster than that of the happening, something definable only with the formula of *non-art*, which includes everything that in one way or another, consciously or not, can be considered negative with respect to art. Such a negation must be understood in its fullest, most complete sense, one that includes habitual gestures, natural events, daily behavior, and everyday objects (the latter either left in their original contexts or "saved" in the tradition of Duchamp's ready-made). Even in this sense the passage from the idea of category to the idea of continuity revealed by Higgins appears incontrovertible. In any case, if from a historical perspective it is easy (as we have seen) to find ties with Dadaism and Futurism, it is perhaps opportune to clarify that today it is no longer a question of groups organized on the basis of a shared poetics, but rather on that of a general thrust that brings together artists working independently from one another, and whose contacts are more the consequence than the cause of a shared vision of reality. The last example of a group organized according to the historical avant-garde model could be Fluxus, which has certainly set the stage for any subsequent attempts to abolish the professional status of the artist: as George Maciunas said, in fact, "the artist must demonstrate that everything can be art and that anyone is capable of being an artist." Fluxus festivals were possibly the most convincing and explicit fusion of elements that constitute the response to the unease of the artistic operator in contemporary society, unease that we can see as "experience" in the Husserlian mold, and thus as "interpretation" of such experience. The request for a "simple," "fun" art is born either from an exercise in anti-intellectualism that we can define, with Tzara, as "spontaneous," or from the demand to sever the umbilical chord that links "rare," "precious," "serious" works of art (polemically these adjectives are synonymous) to an increasingly specialized and sectional discourse.

LXXI

Departing for Sicily

```
•   .   .   .   .   .   .   .   .   .   .   .   •
•   •   .   .   .   .   .   .   .   .   .   •   •
.   .   .   .   .   .   .   .   .   .   .   •   •
•   •   •   .   .   .   .   .   .   .   .   •   •
•   ^   .   .   •   .   .   .   .   .   •   •   •
•   •   .   .   .   .   •   .   .   .   •   •   •
•   •   .   .   .   •   .   .   .   .   .   •   •
•   •   .   .   •   .   .   .   .   .   .   .   ?
```

Dear Adriano, digging through some old books I found this text by
Nievo (Ippolito Nievo, Gli amori garibaldini, Tipografia di P. Agnelli,
Milano 1860) that I didn't know, and I believe very few do: it is on page
93. Besides the ideological and formal reference that seems absolutely
romantic to me, the "visual" analogy with concrete poetry is surprising.
It seems worthy to be transmitted through "Tam, Tam." In any case I
send it to you as information. See you soon, *Claudio Parmiggiani*

10/9/74

Claudio Parmiggiani, "Found Poem"

II. Experimental Poetry and Experiments in Poetry

As mentioned above, the preceding considerations have special
meaning with respect to the problematic of total poetry, which is
presented as a vast area of creative research that lives and grows
through a densely-woven network of connections linking all of its
points of reference, both "internal" and "external." If the impulse
to leaves the confines of one's own territory is an established characteristic of the various arts, the art of the word is perhaps involved
in it on a more profound and definitive level in that it attempts
a metamorphosis so radical that the very nature of the imagination is brought into question. In fact, what still survives, its roots
planted firmly in the earth, is a cult of poetry as pure creation, as
closed, privileged, if not "sacred" creation. Although it has to do
with increasingly less-heeded cultural arenas, this superstition is
far from disappearing. New poetry, on the other hand, takes as the
point of departure for its formative process languages typical of
other arts, particularly the plastic arts, to fashion itself as an "object"
that rejects reading. According to Garnier language is no longer a
code for communication, but a material that needs to be brought
to life. With his *evident poetry,* Jiří Kolár takes the realization of this
postulate even further, establishing an effective objectivity of the
"text." In 1961 (the date of the formulation of "the first manifesto of
evident poetry"), Kolár abandoned verbal poetry and began to exper-
iment with then unknown techniques in a space of relationships,
whether previously existing or yet to be created, between the poetic
text, collage, and object. Works of evident poetry, created with the
aim of being universally "readable" (some were dubbed "illiter-
atograms"), were founded on the primordial elements of visual

communication. These experiments included the covered cobble-
stones of enigmatic signs, "lunograms" or "scriptures of madness,"
and object-poems in which words were replaced by small objects
arranged line after line. According to Šmejkal, a similar form of
visual poetry had been attempted in Paris in the 1950s by the Czech
Surrealist poet Jindřich Heisler. Kolár is dominated by an obsession
with the particular: smudges of ink, fragments of musical scores,
matches, garments, maps and innumerable other finds brought
to light by the subterranean world of the quotidian comprise an
inexhaustible inventory. But Arrigo Lora-Totino is correct when he
maintains that in this case an inventory cannot not be an empirical
reorganization "overturned" by absurd gags in a type of "homeo-
pathic geometry," that is, an anti-romantic proposal of minimum
choices and modules. Nothing is omitted or rejected from the field
within which material enters into "a relationship of attraction/
repulsion" with humanity.

In any case, I would say that the first name in modern poetry
to be identified with research into the visual transformation of
poetic composition is that of Rimbaud, though many feel Rimbaud
is to a great extent responsible for the mystagogic stance present
in so much of the poetic production of our century. In reality,
this responsibility must be attributed to a certain type of critical
reading oriented more toward myth than toward a careful revela-
tion that what is new is not so much "formal" as it is "technical."
In the famous sonnet "Voyelles" ["Vowels"], Rimbaud attributes
fixed chromatic responses to vowels, following, as Carlo Belloli
has said, "an instinctive desire to create a synthesis of poetry and
painting." In 1915 Robert Delaunay sought to interpret Rimbaud's
sonnet visually, with a watercolor that is still useful today for
understanding not only the more or less conscious intentions of
the greatest of the *poètes maudits,* but also the later interest many
painters took in a form of abstract "writing." In fact, we can refer
to the example of Delaunay – without, however, forgetting the
introduction of typographical characters in paintings by Cubists
and by Schwitters, Picabia, Severini, and others – to evaluate the
meaning of pictorial composition based exclusively on the use
of letters, whether alphabetic or not (often similar to ideograms

and hieroglyphics), in Klee, Miró, Tobey, Novelli, Cy Twombly, etc. Otherwise, as we have already had occasion to note, painting constitutes a constant point of reference for visual poets, and not only on a level that analyzes theoretical relationships and practical possibilities, as in the case of Gomringer and Max Bill, for example, but also on a more straightforwardly visual level. The latter is evident in the well-known series of "homages" to various painters (Albers, Brancusi, Burri, Dubuffet, Fontana, to name a few) in which Jiří Kolář composes typescript texts, each of which contains only the letters of the painter's name, with repetitions, variations, and superimpositions such that the result corresponds to the style of the cited author, from Dadaism to Abstract Expression, from abstraction to Duchamp.

Evidently the basic problems of this new poetry only acquire meaning if placed in proximity to the basic problems of other sectors: thus it is not so much the simple convergence of results, but the actual substantial identity of the methodological behavior. And this total opening is itself a method, in that it affords the cultural operator, too often exiled in his chosen craft, the broad possibility of prediction when confronted with the circulation and exchange of projects, when culture increasingly assumes the connotations of a phenomenon disconnected from strictly national spheres and endowed with laws valid almost everywhere. In fact, it has been noted that the first examples of concrete poetry were created almost simultaneously in Brazil, Switzerland, and Italy – by the Noigandres Group,* Eugen Gomringer, and Carlo Belloli, respectively – and the background of the historical avant-garde only partially explains this coincidence. In fact, on the one hand we think of Pound, on the other of plastic concretism or Futurism. The historical avant-garde had already given disconcerting examples of this phenomenon, but it was only after World War II that it began to be repeated more and more frequently, if not to become habitual. Coincidences such as these reveal the identity of deep intentionality. That which for decades had been little more than a semi-conscious

---

* The meaning of the word "noigandres" is unknown and taken from a canzone of the troubadour Arnaut Daniel, traceable to Ezra Pound's *Canto xx:* "Noigandres, eh noigandres, / Now what the DEFFIL can that mean."

effort to step outside the limited field of one's own methodological routine to discover the seed of new impulses in the methodologies of others, can now be considered a conscious road to creation, or even the only road to creation still open. Thus around the world experimental poets work, with vastly different, even contradictory cultural traditions behind them, in directions that are surprisingly coincident.

In this context, what specific meaning can we attribute to the title of our book? In what way can such a title indicate precisely and account for the situation of new poetry? And above all, to what degree does the hypothesis it contains correspond to historical reality? *Toward Total Poetry* seeks to establish the need to see the field of experimental poetry not so much as a confused, fragmentary area in dispersion, but as the coexistence of various lines of march bound up in a dense network of connections and exchanges: "Concrete poetry does not divide languages," writes Max Bense, "but unites and creates them. Its linguistic intention is to have, for the first time, brought about a poetic current that is authentically international."

The numerous forms of experimental poetry are no more than various sides of the same problem. According to an "inventory" edited by Anna and Martino Oberto, experimental poetry can be proposed as: visual, concrete, aleatory, evident, phonetic, graphic, elementary, electronic, automatic, gestural, kinetic, symbiotic, ideographic, multidimensional, spatial, artificial, permutational, found, simultaneous, random, statistical, programmed, cybernetic, semiotic, and as we shall see, the list is growing. Still, many of these definitions refer to isolated endeavors or to the work of groups that existed only briefly. Moreover, "transmigration" from one group to another, from one pursuit to its opposite (or complement), is typical of experimental poets. We will return to many of these aspects and consider them briefly while others will be examined in greater depth. It is clear that we are presented with a "substitutive" aesthetic, one in which various poetics can find a critical systematization based on objective differences between them. As we shall see in the case at hand, different definitions often indicate similar ideas, even if only in their development.

Ladislav Novák, "Individualist"

Such can be affirmed by Luciano Nanni's proposal: "On the structural level, all given definitions appear to agree on a shared distraction from the mind, while on the more semiotic/communicative level they reveal a shared tendency toward evident processes of rapid and estranging operations of code."

The problem is not only to transform poetry into something new compared to poetic tradition, but above all that through this transformation poetry become a total art. New experimental poetry is no longer exclusively interpretable as a force modifying the usual instruments of poetic creation, or as the necessity of overcoming national linguistic barriers to an explicitly international poetry. Today it seeks to become a total medium, to escape all limitations, to include theater, photography, music, painting, typography, cinematographic techniques, and every other aspect of culture, in a utopian ambition to return to origins. This aspiration is realized over time through an inexhaustible series of metamorphoses of the poetic "genre," that Gomringer notes as a prime place for the solution of the problem of "today's perturbed relationship between language and its society and between society and its language." The task of the new poetry seems to be that of rendering sociologically active a linguistic reality that risks remaining "private," and without contact with the world. The triumph of mass communication perhaps coincides with the increasing impotence of the arts, but may also represent a proving ground of its capacity for renewal. While Tristan Tzara's famous "recipe" for making a Dadaist poem (cut out words from a newspaper article, put them in a hat, shake gently, remove the words, etc.) can be interpreted as an invitation to the absurd, it can also be viewed as an attempt to detract from the newspaper, to bring about its rebirth as poetry with a completely altered appearance, that of common spoken language: the absurd is then capable of constituting a means, and not just an end.

Timm Ulrichs: "Montage"

Today the non-conventional manipulation of such a conventional point of departure is a common technique not only in poetry, but also in theater, music, and in the plastic arts (although the meanings of these categorical terms are changing, it is still convenient to use them). Thus we can now speak decisively of total poetry encompassing various distinctions of schools or tendencies that will remain valid and cannot be replaced, except from an exclusively historical and pragmatic point of view. Timm Ulrichs' "total poems," for example, cover a vast zone of experience, from Dadaist-type exercises to visual poems, and from found poetry to the happening. Through the use of a computer, the poems of Carl Fernbach-Flarsheim become structures convertible into other media: architecture, music, design, theater.

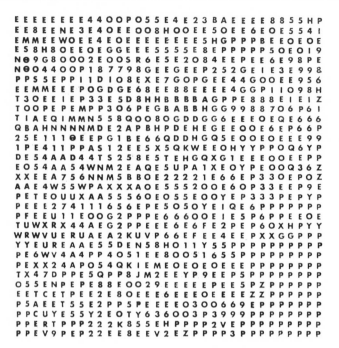

Carl Fernbach-Flarsheim, "Structure-Poem"

In fact, what is occuring here is what happened to literary genres following the war, and naturally not only in Italy: every polemic based on these genres has become superfluous since their actual meaning is found in their encounter and integration. "Visual poetry," says Miccini, "seeks to dilate the field of expression beyond its narrow realm of genre in order to multiply its powers of signification... The encounter, the interaction, the convergence of different semantic areas can open numerous cracks in the jealous universe of poetry, just like in music and painting." The Belgian magazine *Labris* can serve as an illuminating example of this proposition. *Labris* was born from the desire to reunite the two poles of contemporary avant-garde poetry: the "subjective" (jazz-poetry, action writing); and the "objective" (concrete, spatial, serial, visual poetry). The "objective poets" of *Labris* are Leon Van Essche, Ivo Vroom, Pierre Anthonissen, Michel Le Clerc, and Laurent Veydt.

Hugo Neefs, one of the founders of the magazine, suggests setting aside the problem of the possible (or impossible) synthesis between the two poles, maintaining that the poetic text must be considered "autonomous." At any rate, these distinctions have an operative value not only if we regard them from the broader perspective that takes the present (or future) into account, but also if we pay attention to the recent past. Because, in fact, beyond the distributions of territory carried out by and relating to the historical avant-garde, we find a common denominator that becomes increasingly clear the farther from it in time we go. It is as if for many years a large number of branches sprouted from a single trunk, whereas now the tendency is to see the reunification of the many into a new whole. An international exhibition organized in Paris by Julien Blaine collected works from widely varied origins under the label of "elementary poetry." The common denominator can likely be found in an elementariness proposed as the refusal of an artificial privileging, both intrinsic and extrinsic, of literature. New poetry seeks direct contact with the public, wishing to become, in the words of Gomringer, a "useful object," and in doing so can only attempt to eliminate all of the mystifying superstructures – from the crude concept of "exceptionality" to the more subtle but similarly pretentious concept of "commitment" – that invalidated the relationship between the historical avant-garde and society.

Experimental poetry also plays a role in the process of overcoming the inheritance of partialities and polemics that the historical avant-garde transmitted to the post-war avant-garde. This inheritance is not only interwoven with solid reason, but also with sophistry born of the need to distinguish itself at all costs – in a competitive situation dependent on the specific condition of the intellectual in bourgeois society – from movements or groups committed to multiple aesthetic directions. This battle between *pares* was conducted with the same methods and violence that characterized attacks against traditional culture, and the radical negation of the *mores maiorum,* one that displaced the battle from the vertical to the horizontal plane, did not always reap truly positive results with regards to liberating art from the ideological impediments of the past. The return to a unity in variety is in no sense a way to suffocate the vitality of the assorted tendencies and personalities. Instead, it is easy to realize through an objective observation of the experimental poetry phenomenon, in both the historical avant-garde and the post-war avant-garde, that only with a certain degree of difficulty could they bring back the experiences of a shared ideal. In reality, if we speak of total poetry as a fact that is coming into being it is because this shared ideal has already been expressed in works and theoretical texts of the most recent and advanced poetry. And it is in this sense that it is possible to welcome the invitation of Vincenzo Accame to no longer speak of "experimental poetry," but to discuss "experiments in poetry." As a result, that aesthetic level which is still dogmatic and constricting is replaced by one that allows work to progress freely on the plane of "interactive poetic techniques." Accame insists on the possibility of a global effort, based on the shared intent to attain an integrality of poetic gesture. Even Pierre Garnier's Spatialism puts forward the fusion of various tendencies in a single organism based on the objectivity of creative techniques and the elimination of the boundaries separating literary genres. In particular, Garnier tried to advance the idea of theater-poetry (or of poetry-theater): "There is no difference between poetry and theater, because the poet is also a director. This is obvious in the phonetic poem "Entrance" by Seiichi Niikuni: it deals with the theatrical montage of questions and answers, words, vowels, and consonants that are spoken by actors and recorded on tape."

Instead, according to Klaus Groh, in an anthology of visual and concrete poetry one must not be concerned with poetic texts but with "forms of communication," starting from the presupposition that such forms of communication are "identical to their interpreta-tion" and considered in opposition to all forms of communication in which the message is not completely consumed. Moreover, one must comply with criteria of experimentation, theory, game, model, demonstration, reduction, interference, permutation, dispersion, series, structure. The scope of possibilities is evidently quite vast and in practice includes all or almost all of the variants related to the text understood as an autonomous examination of the relation-ships between linguistic material and extra-linguistic mechanisms,

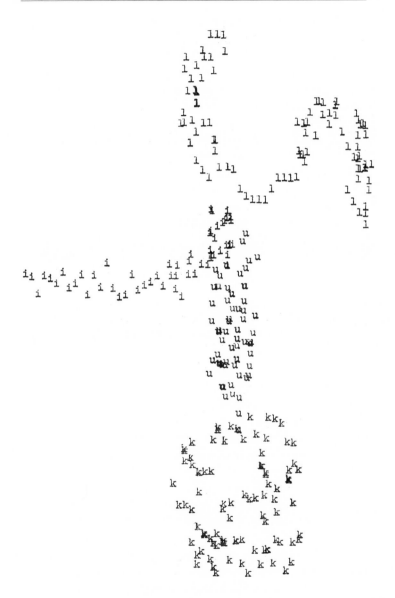

Ilse & Pierre Garnier, "Spatialist Text"

provided that these relationships do not under any circumstance undergo metaphorical alterations. In the introduction to *The Word as Image,* Berjouhi Bowler maintains that visual forms of writing must be considered through a lens that keeps even the most ancient Western and Eastern civilizations in sight; since in the majority of the cases, ancient texts present explicit ties with magic, religious rites, or superstition, we realize that the demand for a relationship with the Logos, "the word incarnate," often appears. Bowler's research originates in the Far East, and moves toward an international movement of concrete poetry. The anthology is geographically based, but within this criteria there is a progression from the amulet to the prayer to the poem. This progression does not stand apart from recognizing the appearance of a desire to "revive the All-Knowing God killed by Nietzche" as a necessity for unity, integration, and omnicomprehensive synthesis. Therefore, the concrete poem seems to arise not only from the necessity for a rehabilitation of the word, but also from the impulse to provide new guarantees to individuality (not by chance does Garnier maintain that man is becoming a cosmic being and that his poetry must, therefore, be at a universal level). In *The Word as Image,* the recent internationalism of concrete poetry is considered almost as a repetition, on the largest scale, of the same phenomenon exemplified by Arabic image-texts written during the period of the major expansion of Islam, from North Africa to Turkey, from India to Persia. In quite the same manner, the Masoretic Hebrew texts originate in both Europe and the Middle East.

According to Emmett Williams, his anthology of concrete poetry would not need to be presented or justified to his readers, since, if "poetry makes poets," then concrete poetry makes concrete poets. In any case, the stress should fall more on the word "poetry" than on the adjective "concrete," in that the opposition between "concrete" and "abstract," according to an analogy consistent with the visual arts, would end up pointing out the iconographic aspects of the phenomenon to the detriment of its specifically linguistic qualities. For Williams, it is inappropriate to impose on the reader the "preconcept" that concrete poetry exclusively constitutes a return to the poetic text as an image. The historical points of reference (from *carmina figurata* to the permutational cabalistic poems) are little more than the confirmation of a reality that has always existed, and the prehistoric graffiti that naturally preceded writing are, in the end, a paradoxical example of this.

Emmett Williams, "Asemantic Permutational Text"

An exhibition curated by Luigi Ballerini, "Scrittura visuale in Italia 1912–1972" ["Visual Writing in Italy 1912–1972"], recently offered a systematic version of the itinerary taken by visual forms of Italian poetry from Futurism to today, without any solution of continuity, unless for obvious reasons we ignore the year 1940 as a chronological watershed. For us, the end of the historical avant-garde coincides with the decisive disappearance of an occasionally naïve, occasionally dangerous radicalism whose best results are purified by a series of confusing compromises with the dominant ideological values. But that which Ballerini defines as the "collapse" of the historical avant-garde does not prevent the exhibited material from being naturally organized as an autonomous category, accelerating the frequency of confrontations and critical cross-references useful to a global evaluation of the phenomenon.

We are not dealing with a superhistoric autonomy, but an autonomy of genre, and a discourse on the visual forms of poetry can (and not only in a preliminary approximation) be stripped of every obvious polemic on "content," for an objective analysis of the structural motivations of the text. So Arrigo Lora-Totino's recovery of certain Futurist directions is historically combined with the interest, typical of concrete poetry, in the mechanism of the word. Nevertheless, not even this method of analysis is immune to mistakes, especially if the intention is to apply it offhandedly. One example is the phrase with which Sanguineti frees himself from the problem in his *Poesia del Novecento* ["Twentieth-Century Poetry"] by affirming that Govoni's *Rarefazioni e Parole in Libertà* ["Rarefactions and Words-In-Freedom"] could be considered, "and not only for these years, the only authentic document of fully realized visual poetry." In this case we must not so much refute the fact that a historical perspective is ignored – Govoni's book dates from 1915, while the term "visual poetry" was coined at the beginning of the 1960s and cannot be tied in this way to Futurist freewordism – as the fact that in speaking of an "authentic document," one is speaking to the reader like an antiquarian. In fact, visual forms of poetry constitute a complex of compositional techniques that accompany and enrich the chronicle of the greater part of the problematics of our century (and not only in Italy, as we all know), from the crisis of free verse to the theorization of poetry "made for the eye." Hence the significance of Ballerini's thesis that the phenomenon of visual writing must be tackled on two fundamental lines: one "vertical" and more precisely descriptive of the historical development of various components, the other "horizontal," that deals with the ways in which poetry has surpassed the specifically literary limits to interacting with the other arts. And I would say these two proposals can overlap without ever excluding one another, so as to offer a third hypothesis, namely that of evaluating along which lines of development poetic language manages, once freed from the linear model, to reveal its own structures. It is a theorem

that has found its most marked affirmation in concrete poetry
(which, on the contrary, in certain cases is also defined with it), but
could also be advantageous for the clarification of other tendencies.

After all, the works of painters like Baruchello or Parmiggiani
and musicians like Bussotti or Castaldi reveal a different context
within which the leitmotif of visual writing can be observed irre-
spective of any poetic dimension, on the contrary decisively taking

Seiichi Niikuni, "Concrete Text"

the path of an a-categorical paralanguage. Chiari's position may
seem eccentric: having abandoned the score, every problem of
notation considered as it would be from a Fluxus perspective or

from that of Simonetti, whose *mutica* (silent music) becomes a mental rather than a visual exercise. A watershed more enunciative than chronological can thus be proposed, establishing the moment in which an operation comprising the "evisceration of language" (we think of Balestrini's "evisceration of history") can result from evidence that has not been compromised or denatured by "practical" conditioning when confronted with "common" codes, and the oppression of advertising in the first place. And it goes without saying that certain garishly "figurative" tendencies can barely tolerate such study, limiting themselves to an "annotated" reprint of a certain pop art. The experiments in abstract objectivity prophesied by Diacono are doubtlessly more "committed," especially for the adhesion of the graphic sign to the semantic play elaborated in part according to Joyce's directions in *Finnegan's Wake*, and in part, ultimately, with an accentuated tendency toward the ideogram. On the other hand, it is not only in this case that the destruction of the linear model does not coincide with that "renunciation...of a task of ideological demystification" of the "pluridimensional means of mass communication" that Fausto Curi considers inevitable. A position of this kind overlooks the fact that visual forms of poetry can be evaluated as a permanent element of crisis in the passage toward completely extra-literary phenomena, to painting (naturally), to the happening, and now to behaviorism or videotape. Rather than being considered simple deviations from the literary norm, this deviation constitutes a polemical moment in the foundation of an alternative, not a persistent fact. Note how *An International Cyclopedia of Plans and Occurences* organized by Davi Det Hompson was made possible thanks to alternative channels of information of "phantom" organizations unrelated to the official circuit of information: Fluxus West, New York Correspondence School, Image Bank, and above all, the International Artist's Co-op.

If Ballerini is primarily interested in an "organic" visual writing, from the idea of an "écriture déchirée" we get "Hors Langage" ["Outside Language"], an exhibit that Jacques Lepage organized as an illustration of our progress into that territory situated beyond the confines of national languages (an area he feels has yet to be "invented"). We know that one of the initial objectives of experimental poetry – concrete, visual, or phonetic – was to surpass linguistic customs offices to create "universal" instruments of communication. It is a utopia rigorously pursued by those poets engaged in the creation of "open codes" that present unsolved problems even for linguistic terminology. The *hors* of "Hors Langage" is much more than a simple invitation to "expatriate," in that it emphasizes the situation of a language, "brisé par l'exploitation de ses virtualités" ["shattered by the exploitation of its virtualities"]. In the introduction to the catalog, Lepage summarizes a number of directions that serve to situate the exhibition in the perspective of this problematic. One of the extreme cases, for example, is the apparent inarticulatability of texts that are composed isolated letters, but "even isolated letters," writes Lepage, "insert themselves in the corpus whose semiology has yet to be invented." In support of this thesis, Lepage cites a study by Yvan Fonagy – *Le langage phonétique: forme et function* ["Phonetic Language: Form and Function"] – in which phonetic metaphors are analyzed. Fonagy demonstrated that, even to the blind and the deaf, the stimulus of articulation distinguishes certain "particularities" of alphabetic letters: the *r* and the *k* have a harder sound than the *l* and the *m*, and the *r* is imagined to be a man, the *l* a woman; *i* has a feminine tone, and *u* a masculine one. It is one way of objectifying signs in direct relation with the unconscious, and "Hors Langage" makes this thesis its own in order to propose a path that may permit poetry to flow into gesture (pure or conceptualized). It is clear that from the standpoint of gesture (pure or conceptualized) it is easier to move toward spectacle-poetry, as what we saw in "Experimenta 2," an exhibition curated by Francisco J. de Zabala in Madrid a few years ago. As for this problematic in general, one can easily consult *ccV TRE:* a reprint of the famous magazine by the Fluxus group, published in New York from 1964 to 1970 by George Brecht and George Maciunas. *ccV TRE* (the original format, maintained here naturally, is 43 × 57 cm) can be read and appreciated, first of all, as a Sears & Roebuck catalog (the American headquarters of mail-order sales), but also as a parochial bulletin, a family photo-album, a do-it-yourself guide, or more generally, as a *fin de siècle* poster ruined by dust and humidity.

The technical leitmotiv is the collage, a collage that is "cold" but not "systematic," with elements that are apparently discordant (and often with a certain violence) grounding themselves in a linguistic model that presents itself as capable of going beyond language itself. *Non-art* and *total art* are opposite but complementary extremes of Fluxus discourse, if by "art" we mean a medium endowed with its own internal rules and adept at its own functioning, a circularity of self-sufficient propositions. To say that Fluxus stems from the refusal of a certain Dadaism – in which the work of art maintains those measurable and marketable characteristics of physical objects – in order to choose its "absolute" or "mental" side, doubtlessly helps us read *ccV TRE* without the paradoxical equivocation of trying to concoct either story or summary from it. Certainly, a list of names – Ben Vautier, Higgins, La Monte Young, Filliou, Cage, etc. – can at the very least invite the reader to deepen the Fluxus problem, if we want to consider Fluxus as a problem to solve and not, as seems wiser to me, *a solution without a problem.* So if art as a circularity of self-sufficient propositions is "useless" (Ben Vautier), all we have left are gestures, and immediately following, "the idea in its pure state." Do we take for granted that "self-sufficient" is equivalent to "tautological"? We'll leave the problem of tautology open as a problem of the comparability between tautology and logical discourse. Let us try to consider up to what point today, in the availability of logical discourse and of its acquisitions, are we able to recuperate pragmatic certainties: I would like to say certainties that have, also in the sense of Husserl's immediacy, a response in existence. And the collage in *ccV TRE* is both diachronic and synchronic when put to the test of "the idea in its pure state," precisely because its immediacy does not require explanation; it is reality that slips by on its own as soon as certain mechanized means in common use, the typewriter or camera for example, have "immortalized" the lack of meaning.

In presenting the 1973 exhibit "Verso una terza dimensione della scrittura" ["Toward a Third Dimension of Writing"], Carrega maintained that he preferred the term "writing" to avoid equivocal connections with the term "poetry," whose relationship with the problems and techniques of visualization smacks of the prejudice that sees the word as the only "poetic material," though it has since been established that the concept of poetic material can be freely expanded to include any material whatsoever. At the same time, for writing we must mean "the leaving of a sign on a material that can retain it with the more or less conscious intention of communicating something." Regarding the idea of a "third dimension," it derives from the need to distinguish itself from the two dimensions traditionally recognized in writing "as notations of meanings," the dimension of "content-sign" and that of the "sound-sign." The fundamental role of the eye, in the process of transferring the sign from a visual to a vocal fact, "has always been held to be one of mere functionality in service of the content-sign," be it in the realm of oral culture or following the invention of the printing-press (which ushered in a progressive "privatization" of reading). As a result, the moment arrived to give a proper "social" weight to the "predominance established by the eye over the voice."

Representation, as stated by Clemente Padín in his volume *De la représentation à l'action* ["From Representation to Action"], consists in pointing out an object through a word or image. Though it remains substantially the same, it changes according to the language used, according to the code, and according to whether we are dealing with an image that is either naturalistic, photographic, Surrealist, and so forth, up to the representation of a tree (this object was chosen by Padín for the book's visual introduction) as a symbol of the unconscious in a drawing by a mentally-ill person, a concrete poem by Pierre Garnier, a linguistic pictograph by Agustin Bartra, a support-sktech of analogical forms, as musical code in Respighi's score of *Pini di Roma* [" The Pines of Rome"]. This Padín follows up with what he calls the imposition of determinant elements. In the book's second chapter, he discusses a voyage into the fusion of language and space, one that begins with Simia of Rhodes (300 BC) and his "hatchet" and moves through Rabelais' "bottle," Carroll's "mouse's tail," Valffger's typographical ornamentation (1670), Marinetti's words-in-freedom, Apollinaire's calligrams, Schwitters' sonatas, Werkman's typography (1941), etc., all the way to Lettrism. Then follows the representation of signs (third chapter): after the great wave of the historical avant-garde we have concrete poetry that works on the text's structure, visual poetry that is a graphic formulation of meaning, and phonetic poetry that is an audio formulation of the same meaning. Pop art, the happening, conceptual art, and behavioral art accompany these transfigurations of poetry. The names cited by Padín are rather interesting here, in that we go from Lewis Pazos, who utilizes the meaningful unities of the linguistic system together with meaningless unities of the other system, that of space, to Augusto de Campos who uses the imbrications of one system's meaningful unities in the other system (imbrications seems to be the correct term for all of "classical" concrete poetry) and so on, until the receiver is offered the option of altering the message through the creative consumption of information. In the fourth chapter Padín analyzes how representation is implemented according to different languages providing artists with a single model or theme to develop or vary. Language of action is presented in the final chapter. According to Padín, this derives from the "game" played between the theme and its variations, with the addition of an ideological operation at the level of meaning. Whether this operation is at play in art, comics, behavior, or life, the result does not change; it is the evident contradiction stemming from the fact that information always needs an object to transmit it, be it a piece of paper, a disk, an atmosphere, or a gesture. The circle closes, or seems to close; the path of an experience that is more coherent and appropriate to reality remains open, and upon it the artist seeks to operate directly. The big question remains (that is perhaps Padín's most original contribution to the current debate): which are the meaningless or meaningful unities of the language of action?

Clemente Padín, "Visual Text"

III. *Technological Styles and Total Poetry*

Overcoming personalistic impediments corresponds in reality to a working method applied in practice, and coincides with the need to eliminate the notion of the poet-seer which, as we know, is still tied to Symbolism. After all, the distinguishing feature of our age is no longer just our system of the division of labor (a consequence of the introduction of industrial methods of production), but also the desire for a world in which all socio-cultural differences between the artist and non-artist, as well as those separating the intellectual from his public, can disappear definitively. Total poetry does not offer today's reader a definitive product, something that must be accepted or suffered through in a closed state of perfection; rather, it offers instruments of poetic creation and the reorganization of their structures. The immediate consequence of this new mental dimension is the weakening of stylistic barriers within the field of experimental poetry. The concrete poet, for example, uses words *as* images, while the visual poet uses words *and* images; the former thinks of abstract painting and electronic music, while the latter is closer to the Surrealist tradition of the *poème-objet*. For both, however, what is most significant is the reference to technological culture (and for both, the fundamental style is that which Max Bense calls "technological style"). From this perspective, the undisputed differences that exist between the one and the other can be relegated to the purely technical realm, not as a form of underestimation, but simply to approach as directly as possible the problem of a poetry that, in order to exist, requires prolonged and explicit contact with extra-literary reality. Whatever the position assumed in respect to various expressive devices, the experimental poet begins with the conviction that the old syntactic and grammatical structures are no longer adequate to the thought and communication of our times, and tries to make evident – on the page, or *in any other way* – his resistance to a passive position in favor of a total gesture. This approach is strictly dependent upon the interest in the physical materials with which the text is constructed. "Emotions and ideas," writes Mary Ellen Solt, "are not the physical materials of poetry. If the artist were not a poet, he might be moved by the same emotions and ideas to make a painting (if he were a painter), a sculpture (if he were a sculptor), or a musical composition (if he were a composer)." Thus, for the poet, poetry is predominantly a way to participate in a sociological dimension that is new to the arts, one that makes the arts active with respect to the world.

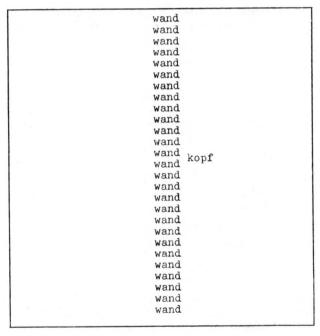

Friedrich Achleitner, from *Quadratroman*

Perhaps the problem will become clearer if we consider the phenomenon of *posters,* which are rapidly becoming a common vehicle for poetic expression. Independent of the technical choice involving the publishable text "from within," in this case the poet builds on an ideological foundation which, by its very nature, is the best demonstration of its affirmation: in fact, the intent of the poet who utilizes a *poster* is to come into direct contact with a public that belongs neither to a club of specialized readers nor to a clan of admirers. The text will be conceived in such a way as to make the semantic content as evident as possible through a formal solution. Nevertheless, the formal solution will always remain in some way antithetical to codified visual languages, since only its difference from the existent iconographic landscape will validate the message and allow it to survive. In the poetry of the Post-World War II era, the poster-poem represents a re-elaboration of the *poème-affiche* whose most noteworthy and useful forms were provided by the historical avant-garde in the works of Blaise Cendrars (1913), Pierre Albert-Birot (1916–24) or Raoul Hausmann (1918), right up to the *affiches poétiques* of Camille Bryen (1934). The competitive dimension in the *poster* is no longer internal to the literary field, but has an "external" relationship with mass media: it deals with an extroversion that is profoundly significant for the understanding of the ideological/aesthetic position of total poetry in society. "The new means of communication," says Gomringer, "participated to a great extent in intensifying the feeling of omnipresence in the individual. While listening to the radio or watching television, the individual recognizes his own eyes and ears, imagining a personal relationship with those things that these elements examine. This fantastic rapport exempts him from distinguishing between possible and impossible, supposition and reality, yesterday and tomorrow. All differences disappear and similarities coalesce into a single entity. The indicative present that predominates in the language of radio and television feigns the objectivity of information that the individual of our time is accustomed to invoke. In doing so, however, one fails to realize the fact that 'objectivity' means a rethinking of the greatest feasible quantity of possibilities, and not the tautological or linguistic reproduction of the existent." Gomringer's *indicative present* immediately makes us think of that *intimation* of the culture of images to which Miccini wants to "respond with another intimation of similar deivces, but with opposite meanings." The totalizing gesture of the new poetry is thus always, in some way, an attempt to involve the reader at all levels, to make him complicit today and co-author tomorrow: according to Solt, the reader, "must now perceive the poem as an object and participate in the poet's act of creating it."

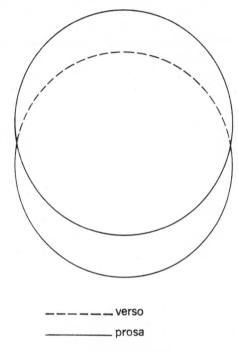

Joan Brossa, "Visual Text"

But the use of the "total poetry" label also derives from the critic's need to avoid stumbling into the many pitfalls that arise from an enormous variety of definitions. If we take the anthology of concrete poetry edited by Mary Ellen Solt as an example, we realize the terminological difficulty that she encountered could have been avoided if "concrete poetry" had been replaced by "total poetry." "There are now so many kinds of experimental poetry being labeled 'concrete,'" writes Solt, "that it is difficult to say what the word means." On the concept of total poetry, one can read Luciano Nanni's notable argument: "In dealing with a totality created by fruition...it too can only be configured as a simultaneous synergistic occurrence of different materials at different structural levels of the text; or, to say it semiotically, of different codes, implying naturally different channels and levels of perception, and, secondly but not in fact secondarily, as a totalizing social practice, i.e. sectors of a vaster and more articulated public." Even Paul de Vree in *Poëzie in fusie* ["Poetry in Fusion"] maintains that those concrete visual and phonetic aspects of experimental poetry are in a *fusioneel* situation, a concept undoubtedly analogous to that of totality. Both his article and the anthology take into account the divergences and points of contact between the various movements which are considered primarily as a theoretical/practical reality, organized around passwords that are neither static nor fixed, but in continual evolution.

a rose is everywhere

a rose

as a rose

for ever is

a rose

for ever everywhere

a rose

Paul de Vree, "Concrete Text"

On the issue of visual poetry, the problem does not change: "When choosing those works to be designated as visual poetry," wrote Lamberto Pignotti in the introduction to his anthology, "I aimed to select that type of poem which in some way tends to relate the word to the figural image or to make verbal material and visual elements coincide. That is why I proposed to exclude the pure experimentation of graphic poetry, even if I must admit that the boundary between the two kinds of experiences is not always evident." According to Mike Weaver, however, it is worthwhile and possible to distinguish three types of concrete poetry: visual poetry, based on the optic medium; phonetic poetry, based on the audio medium; and kinetic poetry, based on movement. From the perspective of individual studies, two currents exist within these three: the first is tied to the Constructivist tradition, the second to an Expressionistic approach. In the first case, the poet arranges the verbal material according to a "rigid" design that he has either invented or chosen, while in the second case, the material (verbal or not) is organized according to an intuitive structure not beholden to any scheme. However, one could say that the excessive use of the generic term "concrete" complicates an already complicated situation. Décio Pignatari, for example, maintains that, "concrete poetry is in strict opposition to any form of Surrealism or Expressionism"; and Ian Hamilton Finlay has defined some of his poems as both "Fauve" and "Suprematist."

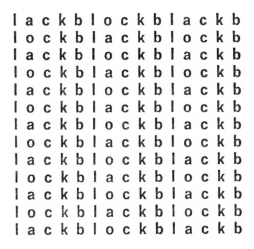

Ian Hamilton Finlay, "Concrete Text"

Instead, what would be desirable is the terminological simplification called for by Heissenbüttel in his "For a History of Visual Poetry in the Twentieth Century," which up until only a short time ago was the authoritative text in Italy, aside from the article "La componente visuale-tipografica nella poesia d'avanguardia" ["The Visual/Typographical Component in Avant-Garde Poetry"] by Carlo Belloli, though the latter was published in a "design," not a "literary" magazine. The term "visual" is used by Heissenbüttel to indicate the vast area of experience (naturally comprising concrete poetry) considered in its entirety, but with a particular insistence on the period of the historical avant-garde. It is a stance taken in order to re-evaluate that period, with respect to the many "innovators" who pretend to ignore it or to have never taken it into consideration in their work, even though his article is devoid of polemics. The disproportionate favor given to the "founders" of visual poetry techniques I find justified today by a series of circumstances revealed to be counterproductive by any accurate analysis, be it a diachronic or synchronic examination of the phenomenon at hand. The fact that Heissenbüttel does not take a stand for any single poetry when presented with the ideological/aesthetic multiplicity of visual poetry corresponds to an attempt to retrace the various models of graphic production within the experimental thematic. Less nuanced is the position of Dorfles, who writes: "one of the *traits d'union* between those specifically concrete compositions and many other visual poems is the attentive urgency that researchers demonstrate when approaching a type of communication through words that is as directly possible as it is visually immediate." Or that of Gomringer, according to whom, "today's concrete poetry is a generic notion that brings together many poetic/linguistic experiments whose chief characteristics consist of a dutiful close examination of the material and its structure, material as the sum of all signs that serve the purpose of poetic construction." Effectively, the tendency toward a fusion of technical procedures of diverse origins was already apparent, even in isolated cases, toward the end of the 1930s. Nevertheless, it is only with World War II that we can perform any premeditated reevaluation of the compositional methods used by the historical avant-garde and of their conscious re-elaboration in the direction of total poetry.

Heinz Gappmayr uses the term "visual poetry" only to establish the essential differences between it and "traditional poetry." These differences can be summed up in this way: in the case of traditional poetry, we have nature, individual experiences, and memories as a point of departure; with visual poetry, however, there is the concept and its signs. In the first case, language is articulated in sentences or phrases and in stanzas and sequences of stanzas according to a variety of conventions (up until free verse); in the second, the form of language is based instead on the isolated noun, verb, clauses, adjectives, adverbs, and syllables: the syntax is either missing entirely or is "demonstrated" in the usual sense. Visual poetry completely abolishes symbols and metaphors, which have a determinant weight in traditional poetry. The latter gives no importance to the external aspect while the form and content of visual poetry derive from elements like color and the placement of letters, the dimensions of the page, even the quality of the paper.

Heinz Gappmayr, "Concrete Poem"

For Gappmayr, the *written* word is simply "a series of straight and curved lines upon a determined surface in a determined space," while the *pronounced* word is "a series of sounds, i.e. audiowaves with determined physical qualities." We are dealing with a clear ambivalence made visible by concrete poetry, but that corresponds in some way to that "open" ambivalence which the use of desemanticized typographic values has made common with a progressive, if not absolute, elimination of the phonic aspect of the word. If Gappmayr's thesis seems to enter at least partially in the Bensian idea of concrete poetry as "triadic function," recent experiences have above all emphasized writing itself. For instance Marko Pogačnik says that even Biljana Tomić considers it linked to a problem of amplification of perception through the addition of seeing and hearing: "Texts are made of letters, letters are made of lines, and lines are there in order to signify determined visual signs in the form of letters"; and it seems to me that here the circle closes to demonstrate, perhaps absurdly, that this ambivalence is still unresolved.

For Max Bense, the difference between a visual and a concrete text should be understood in relation to the concept of a "material text," in which the use of a word is independent of its extratextual meaning and is instead connected to possibilities that are "functional, structural, and aesthetic" within a linguistic world comprising the nexuses of the text. Hence a visual text is "material" insofar as it is determined by the optical character of linguistic signs, while a concrete text is one in which linguistic elements are utilized in their "triadic function" (verbal, visual, and vocal) in both a semantic and aesthetic way.

ir

o
rio
roi
oro
orior
orion
rionoir
ronronron

ri

Max Bense: "Tallose Berge" ["Valleyless Mountains"]

Beginning with the conviction that the process of creating a poetic text coincides with the poetic text itself, Bohumila Grögerová

and Josef Hiršal gave us, with *Job Boj** (1960–62), a full and
systematic recognition of the linguistic mechanisms at the core of
concrete poetry to be used as a litmus test for dealing with social
language and its habitual runaway behavior, at both the literary and
quotidian levels. The book contains twelve chapters, each exploring
a specific sector and summarizing arguments that seem to be
extremely indicative for us, even above and beyond the operation
itself. These are: a) the birth of a text, b) grammatical texts,
c) logical texts, d) stochastic texts, e) syngamic texts, f) intertexts,
g) objectivity, h) proverbs, i) musical scores, j) portraits,
k) micrograms, l) constraints.

```
já :ty já :ty já :ty já :ty já!
já :ty já :ty já :ty já? tyty!
já? ty! já? ty! já? ty! ty!
já! já! já! ty? já! ty? já!
ty ty! ty ty! ty ty ty! já?
já! já! já! ty? já? ty? ty?
já? já? ty ty ty! já :ty já!
já :ty já :ty já :ty já :ty já!
já?! já??!! ty! ty! tytyty!
já? tytytytyty!!!!!!!!!!!
```

Josef Hiršal and Bohumila Grögerová: "Lite"

According to Gappmayr, on the other hand, concrete poetry
consists of the appearance of the "fundamental ontological structure of being" in the concepts and signs referred to by these
concepts, insofar as language deprived of symbols and metaphors
abandons "its function of mediation." If symbols and metaphors
are *abstract* linguistic forms that refer back to objects of perception, the *concrete* text makes it so that the concept appears "in its
nature of concept." Williams as well believed that the authors
who produced concrete poetry in the 1950s were not interested in
looking for an intermedium between poetry and painting, something that occurred later on. Rather, the visual element of the first

---

* [The first word of this title, which does not exist in Czech, is the inversion
of the second word, which can mean "action," "combat," "conflict," or
"struggle."]

concrete texts tended to be structural, a consequence of the poem, an "image" of the lines of force of the work itself.

Belloli's stance on concrete poetry is certainly dubitative in many ways beginning with the doubt that a term like "concrete" can be transferred from the plastic arts to poetry without any precise philological revision. Although some poems written during the 1940s appear in Gomringer's 1957 anthology, Belloli disapproves of the position of strict adherence to Max Bill's theories on plastic concretism expressed in the anthology. Naturally the attempt to "transfer a method of ideation from one language to another, elevating it to a possible general system of art" was achieved more than once, but in the case of concretism, the theory remains "monolinguistic": "The Cubist visual artists were already forced to define a method of poetic composition from the same name, but Apollinaire succeeded in convincing them of the impossibility of adapting a problematic of space to new forms expressing time." In a note from 1959, Belloli scolded concrete poetry for using an arithmetic of the construction of monotonous, bewildering key words without any necessary relationship to typographic/visual structuring, in contrast with the "mathematics of semantic/morphological structures" which stand instead at the origin of its texts. Refusing to be defined as a "concretist," he furthermore believed concrete poetry to be a vehicle for spreading semantic/structural methods and semiotic/typoserial correlations that he adopted in *Testi-poemi murali* ["Mural Poem-Texts"] (1944), *Tavole visuali* ["Visual Tables"] (1948), and *Corpi de poesia* ["Bodies of Poetry"] (1951).

Some ten years after these polemical statements, however, Belloli would give credit to "Concretist" poets for never having entirely neglected the necessary relationship between semantic structures and semiotic structures; but in so doing the practicing verbal Concretists came to identify themselves more and more with the praxis of visual poetry "in such a way as to now render inoperative every critical attempt to deem Concretism a specific tendency in the field of linguistic visuality." In fact, visual poetry surpassed the concept of the ideogram as an "analogy between image and word," creating an "equation between the rhythm of typo-visual structure and the word." This suggested to concrete poetry new possibilities for proposing poem-texts "as combinatory/permutational systems of compact redundant and visualizable linguistic blocks." Today, visual poetry can thus consider itself the "protagonist of a new situation offered to general linguistics in order to resolve informationally the semantic/semiotic quotients of lexical structures with serialistic-permutational links." On the other hand, even Gomringer maintains that Max Bill's theory of concrete art is by no means completely applicable "to linguistic figures," accepting instead, and without reserve, his concept of the functional aesthetic object: such a concept is useful for the "examination" and "clarification" of the instruments of language, "any language" which, according to Gomringer, corresponds to the intentions of modern linguistic science.

For Ballerini, the critique of the "broad" meaning of *concrete* forces Belloli to invoke a "strict" meaning of the visual. It would mean using such a term exclusively to indicate an "optical extension of nexuses inherent in words" (there exists no "intention whatsoever to involve elements external to vocabulary in the attribution of linguistic values"). With regards to critical study, however, Ballerini declares himself open to utilize the term "visual" with a value that is "virtually omni-signaling."

acqua acqua acqua acqua acqua acqua acqua acqua acqua acqua acqua acqua
acqua acqua acqua acqua acqua acqua acqua acqua acqua acqua acqua acqua
acqua acqua acqua acqua acqua acqua acqua acqua acqua acqua acqua acqua
acqua acqua acqua acqua acqua acqua acqua acqua acqua acqua acqua acqua
acqua acqua acqua acqua acqua acqua acqua acqua acqua acqua acqua acqua
acqua acqua acqua acqua acqua acqua acqua acqua acqua acqua acqua acqua
acqua acqua acqua acqua acqua acqua acqua acqua acqua acqua acqua acqua
acqua acqua acqua acqua acqua acqua acqua acqua acqua acqua acqua acqua
acqua acqua acqua acqua acqua acqua acqua acqua acqua acqua acqua acqua
acqua acqua acqua acqua acqua acqua acqua acqua acqua acqua acqua acqua
acqua acqua acqua acqua acqua acqua acqua acqua acqua acqua acqua acqua
acqua acqua acqua acqua acqua acqua acqua acqua acqua acqua acqua acqua
acqua acqua acqua acqua acqua acqua acqua acqua acqua acqua acqua acqua
acqua acqua acqua acqua acqua acqua acqua acqua acqua acqua acqua acqua
acqua acqua acqua acqua acqua acqua acqua acqua acqua acqua acqua acqua
acqua acqua acqua acqua acqua acqua acqua acqua acqua acqua acqua acqua
acqua acqua acqua acqua acqua acqua acqua acqua acqua acqua acqua acqua
acqua acqua acqua acqua acqua acqua acqua acqua acqua acqua acqua acqua
acqua acqua acqua acqua acqua acqua acqua acqua acqua acqua acqua acqua
acqua acqua acqua acqua acqua acqua acqua acqua acqua acqua acqua acqua
acqua acqua acqua acqua acqua acqua acqua acqua acqua acqua acqua acqua
acqua acqua acqua acqua acqua acqua acqua acqua acqua acqua acqua acqua
acqua **incolore** colore trasparente **acqua** percorso voce e voce **acqua** mare goccia
sfera una mano **acqua** verticale cielo una bocca **acqua** piano fiume una casa **acqua**
filo roccia un fiore **acqua** pioggia volto un bimbo **acqua** nubi atmosfera dèi **acqua**
pozzo eco un villaggio **acqua** ghiaccio cristallo un esquimese **acqua** sole foglie una
donna **acqua** barca silenzio un uomo **acqua** cielo medusa luna **acqua** orizzonte
occhio pesce **acqua** nave acqua uomini **acqua** palma sole voci **voci sole palma**
acqua **uomini acqua nave** acqua **pesce occhio orizzonte** acqua **luna medusa cielo**
acqua **un uomo silenzio barca** acqua **una donna foglie sole** acqua **un esquimese**
cristallo ghiaccio acqua **un villaggio eco pozzo** acqua **dèi atmosfera nubi** acqua **un**
bimbo volto pioggia acqua **un fiore roccia filo** acqua **una casa fiume piano** acqua
u**na bocca cielo verticale** acqua **una mano sfera goccia mare** acqua **voce e voce**
percorso acqua **trasparente colore incolore** acqua acqua acqua acqua acqua acqua
acqua acqua acqua acqua acqua acqua acqua acqua acqua acqua acqua acqua
acqua acqua acqua acqua acqua acqua acqua acqua acqua acqua acqua acqua
acqua acqua acqua acqua acqua acqua acqua acqua acqua acqua acqua acqua
acqua acqua acqua acqua acqua acqua acqua acqua acqua acqua acqua acqua
acqua acqua acqua acqua acqua acqua acqua acqua acqua acqua acqua acqua
acqua acqua acqua acqua acqua acqua acqua acqua acqua acqua acqua acqua
acqua acqua acqua acqua acqua acqua acqua acqua acqua acqua acqua acqua
acqua acqua acqua acqua acqua acqua acqua acqua acqua acqua acqua acqua
acqua acqua acqua acqua acqua acqua acqua acqua acqua acqua acqua acqua
acqua acqua acqua acqua acqua acqua acqua acqua acqua acqua acqua acqua
acqua acqua acqua acqua acqua acqua acqua acqua acqua acqua acqua acqua
acqua acqua acqua acqua acqua acqua acqua acqua acqua acqua acqua acqua
acqua acqua acqua acqua acqua acqua acqua acqua acqua acqua acqua acqua
acqua acqua acqua acqua acqua acqua acqua acqua acqua acqua acqua acqua
acqua acqua acqua acqua acqua acqua acqua acqua acqua acqua acqua acqua
acqua acqua acqua acqua acqua acqua acqua acqua acqua acqua acqua acqua
acqua acqua acqua acqua acqua acqua acqua acqua acqua acqua acqua **acqua**
acqua acqua acqua acqua acqua acqua acqua acqua acqua acqua **acqua acqua**
acqua acqua acqua acqua acqua acqua acqua acqua acqua **acqua acqua acqua**
acqua acqua acqua acqua acqua acqua acqua acqua acqua acqua **acqua acqua**
acqua acqua acqua acqua acqua acqua acqua acqua acqua **acqua acqua acqua**

Carlo Belloli, "Poem-Text"

IV. *Alphabet and Calligraphy*

Moving within the concept of total poetry, it is possible to present today's reader with products of the historical avant-garde that would otherwise be lost or relegated to a decay of ontological characteristics and sub-characteristics, or perhaps even to a nebulous chaos lacking clear points of reference. Additionally, the task of the critic who intends to rediscover examples that best lend themselves to the problems of experimental poetry throughout human history is made considerably easier. We can in fact declare that "models" of total poetry are just as observable in prehistoric culture as they are today among so-called "primitive" peoples. There is in effect an extra-literary tradition, which is also of interest to cultural anthropology, set against the specifically literary tradition, even if at this point it is more a question of their integration than their juxtaposition, especially in light of recent developments in anthropological research. In his analysis of the relationship between poetry and painting, Dom Sylvester Houédard cites various types of pre-pictographic mnemonic techniques, like notches, knots, *quipus* and *wampams*. The *quipu* was an object used by ancient Peruvians to count or remember important facts and events: it consisted of a principal chord from which hung a number of variegated ropes, each with its own meaning;[*] the *wampams* were seashell necklaces that North American Indians used as money, ornaments, and votive offerings. Beyond ideograms and hieroglyphics, runic alphabets, contemporary graffiti murals, children's drawings, alchemical formulas, comics, and so on, also belong to the extra-literary repertory.

It is possible to distinguish a diachronic relationship of interdependence between poetry and total poetry that is opposed

---

[*] Kolár is linked to the *quipu*, with the "evident" paraphrases of his knot-poems.

to a synchronic fracture: in much the same way, visual poetry, understood as a transformation of literary content into visual image, belongs as much to an exquisitely aesthetic field representing a certain period of a certain culture as to the greater zone of quotidian writing practice. If for example we compare one of Apollinaire's *calligrammes* with a Kufic text, we can easily measure the distance between the two different meanings of the problem: on the one hand calligraphy has been organized and contrived according to the image intended by the poet; on the other, an authentic writing technique has evolved toward specific forms of visuality according to a tendency we can consider implicit in the writing technique itself.

O BOUTEILLE,
Pleine toute
De mystères,
D'une oreille
Je t'ecoute:
Ne diffère
Et le mot profère
Auquel pend mon coeur
En la tant divine liqueur
Qui est dedans tes flancs reclose,
Bacchus, qui fut d'Inde vainqueur,
Tient toute vérité enclose
Vin tant divin, loin de toi est forclose
Toute mensonge et toute tromperie
En Joie soit l'Arche de Noé close,
Lequel de toi nous fit la tromperie.
Sonne le beau mot, je t'en prie,
Qui me doit ôter de misère.
Ainsi ne se perde une goutte
De toi, soit blanche, ou soit vermeille.
O bouteille, D'une oreille
Pleine toute   Je t'écoute:
De mystères,   Ne diffère.

François Rabelais, "Bottle," from *Gargantua et Pantagruel*

As far as strictly literary models are concerned, the Alexandrian *carmina figurata* are generally taken as a point of departure: from these a path unravels, its essential moments being found in the texts of master medieval calligraphers, in Rabelais' famous ode to the bottle, in the French *bouts rimés* of the seventeenth century, etc., right up to Lewis Carroll who is correctly considered by many to be a true and irrefutable precursor. In the poem that follows (1897), Carroll offers us a notable example of permutational poetry, transforming the word *winter* into the word *summer* through the substitution of one letter in each verse:

```
w   i   n   t   e   r
w   i   n   n   e   r
w   a   n   n   e   r
w   a   n   d   e   r
w   a   r   d   e   r
h   a   r   d   e   r
h   a   r   p   e   r
h   a   m   p   e   r
d   a   m   p   e   r
d   a   m   p   e   d
d   a   m   m   e   d
d   i   m   m   e   d
d   i   m   m   e   r
s   i   m   m   e   r
s   u   m   m   e   r
```

Lewis Carroll

Seventy-years later (1967), Jiří Valoch tackled the same problem by simplifying it, performing the substitution at the syllabic level without worrying about the intermediate meanings of the words. The text is entitled *Promeny doby* ("the change of seasons") and is dedicated to the painter Radek Kratina, whose work develops a kineticism based on an elementary series of changes:

```
jaro
léto
podzim
zima

jato
lézim
podma
ziro
```

53

jazim
léma
podro
zito

jama
léro
podto
zizim

jaro
léto
podzim
zima *

In *Alice in Wonderland,* Carroll creates an inextricable forest of "nonsense," from which emerge innumerable suggestions of experimental poetry. The fragmentation of verse that Carroll uses in some of the chapters of this book will be taken up again, by Cummings for example. "The Mouse's Tail" figuratively reproduces a mouse's tail through the placement of words and the progressive shrinking of the printed characters; a method that recalls everything from Apollinaire's *calligrams* to the emblematic Baroque poem. Recently, Giulia Niccolai explicitly reconnected with Carroll in *Humpty-Dumpty.* Niccolai's poem takes and develops the language of *Alice* with techniques taken from concrete poetry. In this book, Niccolai gives us an exegetic visual interpretation almost solely linked to the content that gets played with graphically according to Carroll's possible or "impossible" indications, proposing a new code of reading.

Another extremely interesting case is that of the Baroque German poet and mystic, Quirinus Kuhlmann. His mysticism involves a profound experimentalism within poetic language set in relation to a universal magic language. Kuhlmann's originality lies in the fact that he attained ecstasy not in silence but through verbal exasperation, returning to the incantatory power of the word. All of this seems to confirm Abraham A. Moles' thesis that "In the empty field of the mystic, because they have more time to waste, men were able to push the unrestrained course of permutation to its limits." And in essence many of these exponents of new poetry are interested in that particularly effective type of composition that is the litany, even if, obviously, in a specifically secular and profane way. What stands out here is an extra-literary tradition, in which one need not see only a list of more or less random coincidences with the outcomes of avant-garde poetry.

Yet the contrary is also true: literary tradition is not enough to explain the position of the experimental poet in relation to the world. With Rimbaud, the poet becomes "responsible for humanity, even for *animals*." He has the task of "making his invention felt, touched, heard," and finding a language that expresses everything, "odors, sounds, colors"... The poet that Rimbaud speaks of is a *shaman:* involved in reality and unreality at all levels, he re-acquires a social mandate, now thought to be lost, by an act of force. This explains the interest in "primitive" music that can be noticed in the phonetic compositions of the Lettrists, which are always based on an elementary rhythm that serves as a background to the sound plot, grumbling stutters, noises, moans and cries.

After all, the Lettrist movement (born in Paris in 1945) began by taking a position that was openly totalizing: its intent was to transform not only the aesthetic disciplines – poetry, painting, music, theater – but other fields of culture as well, like philosophy and science. The taking of an absolute position is easily understandable in the context of French culture as a reaction to the ponderous presence of Surrealism, which had sought, with obvious success, to renovate aesthetic/natural devices in order to act directly upon an ideological/sociological reality.

Strictly speaking, Lettrist poetry is not explainable if Surrealist experiments with automatic writing are not taken into account. The calligraphic gesturality of most texts produced by this movement is in fact in direct relation to a clear desire to liberate the impulses of the unconscious that one might also connect with the constant use of meaningless onomatopoeia. The transcription of sounds that lack meaning (quasi-sounds or quasi-words) constitutes an essential element of this poem by Roberto Altmann:

Oxdahil nie vargdil
jaija voednil erteoul
chnervda dniez chkil,
chnervda dniez chkil
lmouloimo opiou tial
azna znahil
fnienso nomil
ouknajfaz hil... Mouloik kuloik kluiok jdoi
　　　　　　　　fdertizaek
　　　　　　　　deiteribnec louoiu lium
　　　　　　　　fdretza mouloik
　　　　　　　　mouloik jneaille
　　　　　　　　mouloik zneilzmnail

dassda sdaf
dasesda sdaf
qtip hounda!
Aldalinnn
oxdeider
oxidalinnn
sdai ne zver... Mouloik, mouloik jneaille
　　　　　　　　mouloik zneilzmay

optzikeoua
dioum baradioum cabal
optzikeoua
Kai! kai!
mnkai aidera
kai; dkai...
kai; dkai...

　　　　　　　　Mouloik kouloil
　　　　　　　　jdai
　　　　　　　　kouloik ichkna
　　　　　　　　sdai ne szvner
　　　　　　　　mouloik
　　　　　　　　mouloik avzna.

It would be mistaken, however, to take this type of text into consideration without first clarifying that in Lettrist poetry (as in concrete or spatial poetry) the verbal/visual and phonic aspects are strictly interdependent. The poems of Altmann, Maurice Lemaître, Isidore Isou, Roland Sabatier, or Jacques Spacagna can be thought of as realized only once the sound moment and the lexicographic moment are fused completely. The principal instrument for this fusion is the human voice, used in all of its capacities, natural and forced, obviously far beyond mere diction: "The new poetry, based," Altmann says, "on the melodic beauty of combinations of letters, returns to its original material: the human voice." The conception of the voice as material is indicative of the relationship that the Lettrists have with poetic composition, whose chaotic and irregular choral orchestration obtains results of exceptional tonal complexity, so much so that we would not be mistaken to speak of it as a true informal music. In this sense, Lettrist phonetic poetry represents a fascinating proposition of the total type with respect to Raoul Hausmann's Dadaist experience (1918–19), still based on the metamorphosis of pronunciation. With *b b b b,* for example, Hausmann constructs a phonetic poem of rare intensity, utilizing only the letter *b,* which is played out in changeable vibrations and inflections.

The Lettrist text can thus be considered a type of musical score: after all, the score-poem (even if this term was invented only in 1954 by Bernard Heidsieck) is such a common phenomenon in the panorama of total poetry, and exists independently of its audio realization, that is considered only a hypothesis or is entrusted, traditionally, to the will of the reader. This "Lovers' Conversation" by Anatol Stern (1920) reads:

? ? ? ? ? ? !...

A A ak agh akh!!
bee dlin mm
mm

où très-ou-mais-y mais-on
gazon - gazou - zou
zouillis - pas - ou où

MINOU

mignonet coconet nenet net
memenette miette menunette
MIMI BA - MM MM W!
kr trh / ni ni / wr! WRR
aa

Anatol Stern, who can be taken as the principal exponent of Polish Futurism, used a method of transcription here that the

Lettrist movement will theorize and make their own. The attention of the Lettrists is focused specifically on "the art of versification," an area in which one moves from the word, considered
exhausted, to the letter. This is perhaps more apparent in those
works produced during the first years of the movement's life,
which were characterized by an "ascetic" approach to verbal material reduced to the most simplified alphabetic elements. This
phase had been surpassed by the beginning of the 1950s, when
the Lettrists began to use all means of notation, whether acquired
or possible, individual or collective (graphic and stenographic
signs, algebraic symbols, cryptograms, ciphers, and musical notes)
in an attempt to elaborate a sort of *hypergraphy,* or super-writing,
produced to go beyond the limits of the preceding *metagraphy,* or
post-writing. Likewise, in Portugal, Tavares used an ideogram-
like transcription of sounds and noises, going so far as to add
alphabetic signs similar to runes, and this independently of a
direct Lettrist influence. A similar operation was completed, on
the strictly phonetic plane, by Arthur Pétronio: his "verbophonic"
poems are a symphony of words, noises, tone-colors, and rhythms
whose complex orchestration brings about a type of "acoustic
hallucination" (Francis Lovre). Pétronio defines *verbofonie* as "a
verbal and tone-color orchestration through percussion." Its place
in the sphere of phonetic poetry would be "arbitrary" insofar as the
term *poésie* has by now been replaced by the term *poémie,* taken,
according to "etymological truth," from the Greek *poiéma* (here we
could cite Mario Diacono's similar considerations, although they
are different in both context and intent). According to Pétronio,
today there are two roads that lead to the poetic structuring of a
text: the first is that of the *poémographiste* poets; the second, that of
the *poémophoniste* poets. On one hand we have those who "in their
openness to the cosmic dream" engage with "privileged" words to
express "that which is not painted"; on the other, those who with
"the same openness to the cosmic dream" are engaged in "vibrations" that explain "that which is not spoken." But the verbophonic
poet is not one who names, but one who *does,* and the term verbo-
phony must encompass all the forms of *poémie* that eschew the
prison of lexical/grammatical style represented in graphic form.

The Lettrist endeavor stems from the conviction that poetry and painting are the same thing and that the abolition of the word equals the abolition of the point-line-surface triad constituting the basis of abstract art. The Lettrist movement posed the problem of inventing a new table of values based on the letter-sign that sanctions the elimination of the traditional opposition between figurative and non-figurative art in the interest of a truly total art. This position stems from the harsh criticism that the Lettrists leveled at Apollinaire's *calligrammes,* considered to be a pseudo-figurative experience that was somewhat belated with regards to the Cubist painting of the time. It is not for us to weigh in on the accuracy of this judgment; it is enough to underscore the fact that Lettrist painting-poetry performs an operation not unlike that which during those same years was accomplished by abstract expressionist painting: in this sense, then, the Lettrists can be said to be on target. Even Khlebnikov and Kruchenykh, in a declaration of the Cubo-Futurist period entitled "The Letter As Such" (1913) took on the problem of the importance of characterizing individual alphabetic letters through handwriting: in fact, "mood alters one's handwriting" and "handwriting altered by one's mood conveys that mood to the reader, independently of words." Especially as the same must be said of "written, visual, or simply tactile signs as if felt by the hand of a blind man." We've had enough of typeset letters "lined up in a row, offended, their hair cropped, all similarly colorless and gray – these are not letters, they are trade-marks," because "those now talking about the word are saying nothing about the letter."[*]

The letter as "stain" and as "particle" also constitute the point of departure for Blaine's volume *Paragenesi.* Stain become "mythic sign," the particle of an "exploded" geometrical figure, the letter is primarily taken here as an element of magmatic symbology. It stands in relation to a metaphorically erotic atmosphere in which the "transformation of the word" and the "transformation of the world" seem to coincide on the regenerative plane produced by

---

[*] In Vladimir Markov, ed. *Manifesty i programmy russkikh futuristov.* ["Manifestoes and Programs of the Russian Futurists"] (Munich: Wilhelm Fink, 1967). [Our translation.]

the "copulation" of the *i* (phallic letter) and the *o* (feminine letter). Even Miroljub Todorović, founder of *Signalism*,* states that poetry must exclude the word and treat the letter as the essential medium in its atoms (the letters): Signalism proposes to free the energy of language which up to now rermains virtually unknown. Besides letters, even designs, collages, fragments of used keypunch cards, photos, and electronic numbers and symbols are utilized to create Signalist poems. José Luis Castillejo's *Book of Eighteen Letters* (1972) can be viewed as a systematic study of the optical effects obtained by the juxtaposition of letters of the alphabet considered as desemanticized signs. On every page, comprising 15 lines set in a large typesize and generously leaded, Castillejo repeats two alternating letters, one of which is occasionally doubled until each line contains 30 letters and the page resembles a pattern for an abstract embroidery.

Naturally, it would be absurd to speak of an "expansion" of Lettrism, a movement that had almost none of the organizational and promotional characteristics typical of Surrealism. Nevertheless, it is certain that many of the points of the Lettrist program were collected and utilized in a more or less conscious manner, even recently, by visual poets. Thus *O babel* by Adriano Malavasi can be taken as a score-text derived from an alogical vocabulary, invented entirely for its assonance with existing words. Ugo Locatelli's phonograms also exhibit a list of word-noises that are the refusal and destruction of spoken language. In her "graphic reductions," Mira Schendel carries out an operation of pseudo-primitive manual writing that swings between the concentration of the sign and a calligraphic gesture. These elements are also present in the work of Magdalo Mussio, particularly in the book *In practica* ["In Practice"] (1968), where he wishes to show the existence of a synergy between the data present *within* the problem of "writing" and those found *outside,* in the chaos upon which the message is constructed. If Mussio's calligraphy becomes or aspires to become illegible, that

---

* Dealing with a poetry based on the sign, we ought to translate it as "signism," but Todorović informs us that the term is derived from the Latin word *signum,* which makes the problem of translating it superfluous. (*Kyberno* [Belgrade: Miroljub Todorović, Dobrinjska 3/11, 1970]).

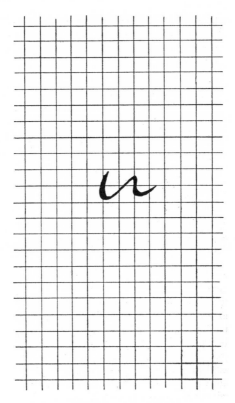

Giuliano Della Casa, "Calligraphic Text"

illegibility is the result of a balance between what Ballerini has defined as the "amanuensis writing" and the iconic absoluteness of any externally detected fragment. This is because communicational reality is external, as remains that type of anti-writing which is, or seems to be, print (even simple photographic reproduction involves the handwritten text in a regressively interrogative alienation). Missing is the Lettristic adoration for hyperwriting; instead we have the sense, attributable to Novelli, of the object-text. Many meters of magnetic recording tape snake and tangle in the images of the *Magnétodrome* ["Tape-o-drome"], a negative phonetic poem that Sitta constructed on the equivalence between

word and silence. Physical circuit and mental circuit become identified in the random and unforeseeable circumvolutions of the
reel, whose function/fiction as symbol is solicited by the frequent
input of "narrative" elements, so to speak (in particular relative
to the environment), into the photographs. This cold, gelatinous
material seems to recreate from life the science fiction structures
of pulsing, exploding electronic brains in some final contact
with objects. Beyond these over-simplified allegories, however,
Magnétodrome should be read as the message of a message: it
can be compared to a pre-pictographic system of communication
with a meaning perceptible "at first sight" in every technologically
advanced culture. In the introduction, Alain Arias-Mission is not
mistaken in asking whether words have any meaning in relation
to an operation intent on deleting the word. Rather, I would say
that he has a perfect grasp of the nature of the problem when he
interprets Sitta's proposal as a "metaphysical negative." But is the
negative and metaphysical correspondence between word and
silence an objective starting point that Sitta follows from page to
page, forced to take advantage of the standardized mechanism
offered by the very nature of the instrument "book"? Or do we
find ourselves presented with a dilated and shattered (and not
recomposed) metaphor for the end of language? In effect, one can
say that Sitta performs an operation of "clearing customs" when
confronted with the entire complex inheritance of the various
forms of experimental poetry, from concrete or visual poetry to
phonetic poetry.

Jean-Claude Moineau's *Lecture rapide* ["Quick Read"] seeks to
provide a thesis demonstrating how a book can be "organized"
before it is read, and how the reader is able to understand the book
as a game "in which one has the illusion of being free to cheat."
The "quickness" of reading derives from the predominance of the
iconographic element in writing, reduced to a few essential and
practical indications as to the "use" of the pages. In reality, however,
the images themselves are almost always *inscribed* within the alphabetic letters or in the forms that result from the removal of those
letters following a procedure that demonstrates the possibility of
integration with the image.

Julien Blaine's subtitle to *WM Quinzième* ["WM Fifteenth"] (1966) is "to put an end to pre-semioticism." Beyond the polemical tone of this phrase, it is not difficult to find a hint of a poetics coordinated with that explosion of the critical and creative problematics centered on the sign that still exists today, in France in particular, with its own specific characteristics. For Blaine, such a problematics comes into being only when the passage from word to sign is total, and the task of the poet consists of describing this passage, visually interpreting its various phases. Thus the typographic verbality (conceived at different levels, with superimpositions and interpolations of characters in type of every dimension) becomes calligraphy, obsessive repetition of a single letter, flight into constant babble, invention of absurd semantic variants, until it is transformed into images, and then into an autonomous sign to be understood as an obligatory outlet for a text suspended between "reading" and "interpretation." This almost maniacal description of the effects that the sign's sickness has had on the word is then condensed by Blaine in dazzling visualizations dedicated to a single word and a single letter of the alphabet, as in the poem "Le fabricant de 'i'"["The Builder of 'i'"] in which towers, cranes, bells, obelisks, chimneys, fountains, etc., all receive the dot of the *i*, becoming monumental signs. Could it be an homage to Schwitters' "i-Gedicht" ["i-Poem"]?

Klaus Peter Dencker takes the perspectival drawings of alphabetic letters made by Hans Lemcker and published in his *Perspectiva Literaria* ["Literary Perspective"] (Nuremburg, 1567) to create combinations of flowery elements, generally photographs with outlined colors chosen in such a way as to provoke a reading of the work from a strongly emotive standpoint: internal organs from the human body, fetuses, skulls (but also models, mechanisms, architectonic details). The meaning of this combination of alphabet and images is that their reading must be identical to that of a rebus, naturally on a plane of allegorical deformation internal to the German language. The dominant visual theme is perspective, exploited on the one hand in a metaphysical direction, and on the other as an idea of the flight of the message toward echoes of the grotesque.

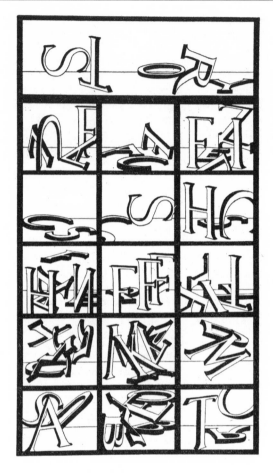

Klaus Peter Dencker, "Text-Bilder" ["Painting-Poem"]

With *Un livre à inventer* ["A Book to Be Invented"] (1962)
Suzanne Bernard seeks to position herself in the field of that "ideal
poetry" that Bachelard defined as "psychic," "mute," and situated
"above the interior word"; once the word is eliminated, the text is
reduced to its essential elements: space, vision, hearing, movement. In other Lettrist-like exercises, Bernard abandons typography
for handwriting, something more pliable and malleable, while the

page is now defined as a temporal, not a spatial unity. The same discussion is applicable to the German magazine *Rhinoceros* (edited by two brothers, Klaus-Peter and Rolf Gunter Dienst). Founded in 1960, *Rhinoceros* collects calligraphic experiments of Lettrist intonation that bring to mind the work of painters like Hartung, Masson, Pollock or Mathieu, even if the word "calligraphy" is often associated as much with the typographic sign as it is with hand-writing. K.P. Dienst interprets the poetic text pictorially, with highly decorative Art Deco results; for his part R.G. Dienst uses a personal and free calligraphy that creates a sort of negative of the poem. In both cases, according to Jasia Reichardt, the visualizing procedure is not an end in itself, but serves as a key to semantic interpretation. What is extremely interesting in this case is the work of Carlfriedrich Claus, who is implicitly connected to Lettrist poetics. Claus' calligraphic texts are born of the interplay between the writing of right and left hands: the right hand represents critical rigor, rational construction, and the analytical moment; the left hand "when writing slips, and semantic value dissolves into handwriting."

For Bowler, the written word was always considered a talisman in the East, and the process of writing was always seen as a magical art connected not only to the technical ability of the calligrapher, but also to his spiritual and moral personality. Even during the medieval period the calligrapher was required to have a certain ascetic quality not unlike those attributable to members of religious orders. Bowler cites the claim of the Persian calligrapher Mullah Mir Ali: "My pen does miracles, and the shape of my words is rightly proud of its superiority over meaning. My pen is the slave of every curve of my letters. The value of each of my signs is eternity itself."

For Arrigo Lora-Totino, calligraphic (and "decorative") effects constitute a significant danger for concrete poetry, particularly in cases where the text does not originate from an effective "discipline of the integrative organization" of verbal, vocal, and visual space. In fact, in concrete poetry the experimentation tends to act "as the organization of the verbal/vocal/visual functions of the chosen language," and such organization must equal a total integration of semantic/semiotic values in exactly univocal structures. Often, however, the visual function is exhausted "in the visualization of a verbal/phonetic movement," that is in the visualization "of a circulation of relationships between one concept and the next," forcing the concrete poem to fall into the status of a "merely literary fact."

Lettrist elements are recognizable even in the phonetic poems of the authors at the head of the magazine *OU*: Bernard Heidsieck, François Dufrêne, G.J. Wolman, and Henri Chopin. These poets take their research to an extremely rigorous level, whether from a theoretical or a technical point of view. In his *crirythmes* ["scream-rhythms"] (1958–1964), Dufrêne exploits the resources of the voice inside and out, while with *L'énergie du sommeil* ["The Energy of Sleep"] (1965) and *Le Corps* ["The Body"] (1966), Chopin experiments with the possibilities of breathing. For Henri Chopin, the Lettrists limited themselves to a "game of phonemes" that must be replaced by a true language of sound: working with the tape recorder, sound poets abolish all forms of alphabetism and rediscover the audio potential of the human voice understood as "song."

```
COUPLET:  HHH  hhh  HHH  hhh  HHH  hhh  HHH  hhh  HHH  hhh  HHH  hhh
          hhh  HHH  hhh  HHH  hhh  HHH  hhh  HHH  hhh  HHH  hhh  HHH
          HHH  hhh  HHH  hhh  HHH  hhh  HHH  hhh  HHH  hhh  HHH  hhh
          hhh  HHH  hhh  HHH  hhh  HHH  hhh  HHH  hhh  HHH  hhh  HHH

REFRAIN:  HHHHHH  HHHHHH     HHHHHH    hhhhhh    hhhhhh    HHHhhh    (bis)
          hhh  hhh  hhh  hhh   hhh  hhh  hhh  hhh   hhh  hhh  hhh  hhh

COUPLET:  hhh  HHH  hhh  HHH  hhh  HHH  hhh  HHH  hhh  HHH  hhh  HHH
                                   etc...

REFRAIN:  hhh  hhh  hhh  hhh  hhh  hhh  hhh  hhh  hhh  hhh  hhh  hhh
                                                                (ter)
```

Henri Chopin, "Hymne international"

In certain cases there can be points of contact between sound poetry and electronic music, but the human voice has wider, more "visceral" registers than the mechanical registrers of electronic music. After all, Berio, Stockhausen and others often used the human voice, either to render their scores richer and more complex, or at least in part to eliminate the "coldness" of electronic sound. Instead, the sound poet never uses sound effects (like those in cinema, for example) or musical instruments: the tape-recorder itself must not be considered anything other than a mechanical means since it "adds" nothing to the voice; the tape-recorder can record all of the possible variations of the human voice, but the voice itself contains the potential of the entire chorus. The only problem is perfecting the consciousness of the poet's "choral resources" that have nothing to do with the practice of diction. With respect to discoveries related to the human voice, Chopin searches for reference points in a field usually considered more solid, i.e. that of written language, citing Brion Gysin's *permutations* and Bernard Heidsieck's *poèmes partitions* ["score poems"], procedures that hover between written and sound poetry. Chopin insists on the visceral quality of sound poetry, emphasizing the mystical ("the visceral expression is to find man"). In this way Dufrêne's *crirythmes* are "above all a human projection." The work of Dufrêne is the pure and simple expression of the human "cry" and finally lays bare how unsuccessful Artaud was in bringing it to completion. The *crirythme* is "a mimetic work, expressive, periodically full of humor, but more often full of anguish. It is a chorus of the mouth and throat."

More graphic than phonic, even Luciano Caruso's experiments in the magazine *Continuum* can be situated in a generically Lettrist sphere. In particular, Caruso's work comes from the crossing of a series of experiences, not all of which are homogenous among themselves, but which are certainly related to the great problem of transforming into writing a Wittgensteinian stance toward language, that often hovers between the gesturality of collage and extreme conceptualization. That is missing however – replaced by an unchaining of semantic assonance – in the intricate calligraphic paths of Emilio Villa.

v. *Typographic Styles*

Perhaps without fully realizing it, the Lettrists remade themselves by modifying a few of Kurt Schwitters' most important theses. In the theoretical text, *Consistent Poetry* (1923), Schwitters argues for the necessity of making poems that utilize only letters: "Not the word but the letter is the original material of poetry ... letters have no concepts. Letters in themselves have no sound, they only offer the possibility to be given sound values." Schwitters' intent is to arrive at an elementary poetry constructed by laying out the page with alphabetic units emancipated from their semantic roots and understood as abstract form, as pure structure. The meaning of the poem is no longer found in the associations of ideas or feelings that it provokes in the reader, but is consumed in the material used. The painting-poem (*Bildgedicht*) does not refer to an external mental reality, but comes into being autonomously as an absolute creation separated from the contemporary context of linguistic and aesthetic conventions. The extreme result of this theory is the "i-Gedicht" ["i-poem"] that consists only of the lower-case *i* with the comment: "read: up, down, up, little dot on top." As Heissenbüttel says, "a banal mnemonic verse used in elementary schools is employed here to demonstrate with this sole example the emptiness of the written surface."

Schwitters' influence on the poetry of the following decades would be decisive: Dieter Roth's typescript concrete poems, for example, clearly take up some of the intentions of the "i-Gedicht." In these texts, Roth renounces the typographic sign for the simpler, more banal typewritten sign, utilizing to aesthetic ends not only the shapes of the letters, but even the artisan-like, temporary, and in some sense "personalized" tone that the text has thus assumed. From these primitive *ideograms,* also published in the magazine

Material (founded in Darmstadt by Daniel Spoerri, Claus Bremer and Emmett Williams in 1957), Roth proceeded toward a progressive complication of the page, which increased year after year, right up to the object-books. What distinguishes Dieter Roth's typescript poems from the "i-Gedicht" is the fact that the letters are often grouped in a more or less random fashion forming islands of meaning. Naturally, Roth was not the only one to utilize the typewriter in this way; actually, it was an instrument commonly used by experimental poets who exploited its graphic potential, achieving results difficult to repeat in typographic composition. The difficulty stems primarily from problems created by the typewriter's mono-width characters, which are different from those of the Linotype. In texts of concrete poetry, they subvert the Linotype's rules of alignment and justification.

Garnier coined the term *poème mécanique* ["mechanical poem"] for texts produced on a typewriter, and he attributed a certain number of distinguishing characteristics to mechanical writing of this kind, velocity being among the most important. At worst, the mechanical text is created as it is typed out, and thus derives from "the almost total elimination of thought, of reflection." The eye becomes the organ that orders and regulates psychic energy, but the procedure remains instantaneous, spontaneous, so that for the author, the work is not the result of any meditation or experience, but of a *gesticulation*. If in handwriting letters pass through the fingers, on the keyboard fingers seek out the letters, and we have a "dance of the hands" that contributes to the pleasure of creation. The latter is no longer a synthesis, that is, a composition based on words and their meanings however distorted and negated, but a "state of genesis" in which the word can be "extended," multiplying at will certain letters and thus moving toward an extension/dissolution of a corresponding semantic value, rendered "baroque" or "classical" (terms used here in their most generic sense) by means of mathematic progressions. Mechanical poetry produces static and dynamic forces, balanced or in movement, within language, whose "functioning" coincides with the text and its meaning insofar as the "lettric mechanism" constitutes the sum or dialectic of the author's psychic energy and the visual energy of linguistic particles. It is perhaps interesting to realize that mechanical writing seems, at least at first glance, to have a number of things in common with automatic writing, particularly when the nearly complete elimination of thought and creative process is emphasized. But at a certain point, Garnier asserts that the elimination of the unconscious becomes necessary, and thus the mechanical nature of the procedure is prevalently "external," connected exclusively to gesticulation. And the term "automation" will be increasingly used in an entirely different sense than that of the Surrealists: as a passage to an ulterior stage of mechanization, a stage in which we shall have the simultaneous construction and destruction of word and letters.

Hansjörg Mayer, "Typoactionen" ["Typoactions"]

There are no islands of meaning in the *typoems* (typographic poems) of Hansjörg Mayer, who uses type as elements of asemantic abstract visual compositions, in which structural tension takes on a new importance in the panorama of today's concrete poetry. Mayer's *typoems* have much in common with the typographic paintings (1930) of the Dutchman H.N. Werkman; Werkman also worked with type for its formal qualities, which are devoid of semantic meaning. In so doing, he activated a space attributable to Constructivism, in which the irregular placement and variety of sizes of the letters introduce a Dadaist note. With *Eyes* (1967), the Canadian B.P. Nichol moved in the same direction, although his texts were not meant to be images, "but syllabic and sub-syllabic messages." Some of John Furnival's poems were created, as was Mayer's *Alphabetenquadratbuch* ["Alphabetsquadratbook"], through repeated typographic superimpositions, resulting in unique visual effects that evoke Gothic stained-glass windows. Claus Bremer, on the other hand, uses verbal material to create an abstract design, though he does not renounce meaning, which is in fact the essential element in his poems. Bremer's texts are real poetic declarations and the visual result is closely connected to their semantic density. According to Arrigo Lora-Totino, in Bremer, as in Gappmayr, there is a strong Structuralist, anti-decorative preoc-cupation, "and by 'decorative' what is meant is the simple causality and lack of transparency, necessity, and intelligibility of the proce-dure's meaning."

Reinhard Döhl, "Pictogram"

Mayer's "typographic style" gives results that lie outside the scope of poetry strictly speaking and engage with the problematics of lettering and design. After all, Mayer was the Stuttgart printer of the experimental series "Futura" and "Rot," the latter directed by Max Bense and Elisabeth Walther, and thus found himself in a situation that facilitated the practical application of his own research. It is not by chance that Stuttgart became one of the most important international centers for concrete poetry. Many poets and designers – Klaus Burkhardt, Sigfrid Cremer, Reinhard Döhl, G.C. Kirchberger and others – gathered around Max Bense, theoretically and experimentally furthering the ideas of this new poetry.

Klaus Burkhardt, "Typogram"

The interaction of poetry, lettering, and design constitutes one of the essential tendencies of concrete poetry.* As Gomringer has written, concrete poetry would rather be linked to architecture, painting, sculpture, and design, than to simple literary commerce. In particular, it is possible to create a direct relationship between

---

* From this point of view, it is certainly significant that Heinz Gappmayr – who with Ernst Jandl and Gerhard Rühm represents concrete poetry in Austria – is a designer by profession.

concrete poetry and advertising graphics since in both cases, the text is elaborated with a method privileging semantic/visual assonances. According to Max Bense, concrete texts and advertising texts are "typographically" close since their aesthetic pattern of communication is nearly identical: "The central sign, mainly the word, assumes the function of a slogan." Max Bense asserts that the rapprochement of poetry and advertising ("in that *generalized form* of literary structure that today is simply called the *text*") was what prepared the linguistic field for the comprehension of concrete poetry. Naturally – notes Sandro De Alexandris – concrete poets have a far greater area of experimentation at their disposal than do advertising designers, whose message is, by the nature of things, generally conditioned by external and extra-aesthetic factors.

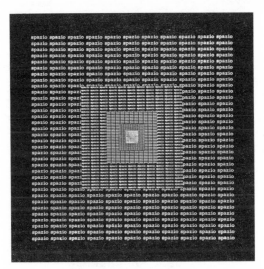

Arrigo Lora-Totino, "Space"

In both cases, however, as Arrigo Lora-Totino writes, "the semantic quality becomes figural, iconic, acquiring a plastic dimension that goes beyond the verbal." In its own way, the iconographic landscape influences the poet, who thus needs to take an unending quantity of images into account. Kirchberger's poems, for example, are based on the integration of compactly geometric colored forms and obsessively repeated writing, with results that make one think of abstract billboards, particularly because of the notable dimensions of the text.

With *L'in finito* ["The In Finite"], "a plastic/verbal situation," Lora-Totino and De Alexandris aim to functionally integrate word and design, a fusion or conversion of the one into the other, and vice-versa, without the absurd waste of space that usually accompanies procedures of this type. Their collaboration moves in the direction of that non-esoteric, but certainly not easily found entity that is, in the form of the book-object or the *plaquette-affiche* ["poster chapbook"], the visible "identity" between sign and meaning. This movement toward a semanticity that is indissolubly connected to graphic expression obviously sets it in relation to the recent tradition of concrete poetry. Yet here the words "finite" and "infinite," which are the *same* words, are repeated until they form a horizon line, ambiguously legible in a simultaneity willed by the eye, as image. Thus, more than a text of concrete poetry, it is a "plastic/verbal situation," a being faced with an untranslatable *déjà vu,* and above all inseparable from a third element (not as yet considered): the material support of the composition that is conditioned by it *even* in reading. The research then seems to turn to the temporal dimension, to the possibility of repetition that is in itself inexhaustible. Or, less dramatically, to the constitution of an invariable ideographic eloquence.

undundundundundund
undundundundundund
undundundundundund
undundundundundund
undundundundundund
undundundundunduńd
undundundundundund
undundundundundund
undundundundundund
zer   br eche   n

Gerard Rühm, "Concrete Text"

Even *Busta celeste* ["Heavenly Envelope"], by the same authors, is a fine example of graphic simplification and the structuring of lyric dictation, as well as an ironically functional integration of word and design. I say "ironically" because, from both a graphic and a lyric perspective, the choice of the play-on-words, "cielo-cieco" ["heaven-blind"] constitutes a voluntary theoretical impasse undertaken as an exercise whose outlet is semantic (visual) rarefaction. The extreme precision of the essential calculation that underlies the text's design is not diluted in its writing, but is predictably strengthened in the end, particularly in the black "blinding" page that seeks to be a deletion, if deletion of the horizon is the keystone to this text.

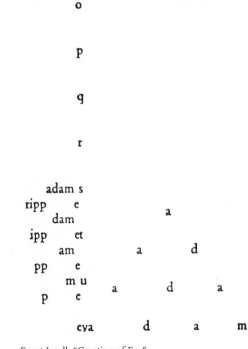

Ernst Jandl, "Creation of Eve"

The comments about Kirchberger on the relationship that can
be established between advertising and poetic texts are also applicable in part to Ferdinand Kriwet's *poem-painting*, although Kriwet
utilizes only isolated letters and sentence fragments that overlap
and intersect on the canvas, in this case of large dimensions, as
on a white screen. Kriwet works on the letter forms, cutting them
vertically and horizontally, alternating their dimensions or breaking
them apart to obtain a type of para-alphabet. The use of clashing
acrylic colors puts a final touch on the optical play in these poems
which, according to Kriwet, "exploit the possibilities of writing in
a productive way – in the general sense of the word – and not solely
in a reproductive way," thus emphasizing the moment of *invention*.
For these large-format compositions, Kriwet used the abbreviation
PUBLIT (from *public literature*), and in so doing underscores the
existing relationship between new poetry and the iconographic
urban panorama. Poetry ought to aim at that public that is habitu-
ally bombarded with "street texts" which, in their effort to reduce
the message's degree of redundancy, recall the actual elementary
ideographic nature of language before phoneticization. The same
process of message simplification and schematization occurs in
"written painting," eliminating the intimacy that characterizes traditional reading and thus casting doubt on the survival of the book
as we currently know it. "The age of the book is still to come," says
Kriwet in fact, referring to the countless unexplored possibilities
of the *object*, considered in most cases to be nothing more than a
passive instrument, deprived of any aesthetic connotations in itself.

The poets editing the magazines *Approches* ["Approaches"] and
Agentzia ["Agentcy"] (Julien Blaine, J.F. Bory, J.C. Moineau, Jochen
Gerz), on the other hand, were convinced that the age of the book
had already come, and that it was impossible to refer beyond its
liberation from traditional use. In fact, the content of the book is
no less important than its appearance, but only from the fusion
of these two elements into a single, inseparable, unique organism
is the book-object born. It must not only be read, it needs to be
touched, handled, dismantled, and reassembled. The reader's
pleasure coincides with the form of the book: the pagination,
cutting, binding, thickness and color of the paper, arrangement of

typographic signs, page-numbering, etc. In sum, these poets exalt the technical dimension of the book in order to reinvent it as an adventure, a game, and to simultaneously lay bare the mechanism of reading.

Focused on this argument, the extensive, elaborate exhibition "I denti del drago" ["The Dragon's Teeth"] (1972), curated by Daniela Palazzoli, considers "the transformations of the page and the book"

Ferdinand Kriwet, "Poem-Painting"

```
                        if you wish make it
                    if you wish make it
                fi uoy wish make it
            fi uoy hsiw make it
        fi uoy hsiw ekam it
    fi uoy hsiw ekam ti
        uoy hsiw ekam ti if
            hsiw ekam ti if uoy
                ekam ti if you wish
                    ti if you wish make
                        if you wish make it
```

Jochen Gerz, "Concrete Text"

implemented by the historical avant-garde and continuing up
to the concrete and visual poetry of the post-Gutenberg era in
which we live, and which we experience as an irreversible alternative. The very cover of the catalog, with its naphthalene coating,
imposes the idea of a book-object (or object-book) to be touched
and smelled. But the strong odor of the naphthalene cannot help
but recall grandmother's blanket chests, and thus the antiquated,
the museum, and the decaying library. The irritating tactile and
olfactory metaphor is open to many interpretations, but especially
to that of a privileged cultural phenomenon whose very essence is
offended by mass media. Does the exhibition aim to be a conscious
challenge to the museum? It seems to me that Palazzoli avoided
this issue because of its irrelevance, resolving it as a pseudo-
problem with a symbolic offering: the catalogue and its cover, in
fact. After all, the exhibition has done more than merely clear the
air of a number of misunderstandings related to the recent fossil-
ization of the controversy. It managed to condense an entire area
on "one of the most institutionalized structures of communication," the book. It is precisely in reference to the table-page and the
book-object that the post-Gutenberg situation poses one of its most
subtle questions. I am referring to the creation of unique, one-off
works that again pose the question of the ideological justification
of an elite product and its survival. It is not by chance that Gianni
Emilio Simonetti's digression on the proto-history of the book as

"gift" investigates an apparently evasive preciousness. Fluxus has certainly proposed a far less rigid path. Its use of the book-object is almost always a "being there" of multi-voice collaboration, where even the printing of multiple copies insures a horizon of random or predisposed variants, which only seems to suggest a non-emblematic "reading" that, though it may be less suggestive, is undoubtedly fuller and freer, more curious and open to invention. However, the emblematic nature of works such as Claudio Parmiggiani's or Vincenzo Agnetti's is obviously a pretext for the metamorphosis of the book-object into a document of silence, and of Fluxus' own maieutic crisis. We can affirm that the well-proven techniques for creating the book-object and the table-page can only provoke a problematic within their very being. By speaking of them as "a model of inclusive perception," Palazzoli reasserts, I think, a type of irreplaceable monopoly towards mass media. An autonomous and self-sufficient world, at least in terms of excess.

If not intended as a challenge to museums, this idea of the book-object may in the first place become a challenge to technological culture. Its emblematic nature is configured as a refusal (be it only a hypothesis), an entire range of values is presented either negatively or positively. It reopens the argument about Wittgenstein and his declarations concerning the lack of meaning of propositions considered to be fundamental, and on the recourse to tautology. In effect the book-object and the table-page only touch upon the paradox inherent in their indemonstrable configurations, referring to an entirety parallel to the entirety of poetry understood as a tension leading toward the totality of knowledge. On the contrary, any assertion placed exclusively on the medium reveals a lack of flexibility justified perhaps by the times, but that the existence of a modern tradition hinging upon Duchamp renders unthinkable. So the works of Gianfranco Baruchello, George Brecht, and Jiří Kolár activate a network of meanings that, to cite Wittgenstein once again, "show" reality without "saying" it. An extremely efficient mental concentration results from this phenomenon, alien to every metaphysics, yet allusive to any "mystery" that may be proposed as an alternative recoverable in everyday things, prior to the museum and mass media, *or after*. This is no ready-made poetics; the "show" without the "tell" is not a linguistic operation, but an experiential imperative. And so the section "Il libro come luogo di ricerca" ["The Book as a Place of Research"], curated by Palazzoli and Renato Barilli at the Thirty-Sixth Venice Biennale, may appear as an expansion of the theme of the exhibition, which was dedicated to behavior. A ritualizing gesturality seeks nothing more, and its role in the consciousness/action equation need not be explained, it is an authentic ambition in itself, and more authentic if it fulfills a role that surpasses the boundaries between art and life.* In its production of a global stylistic organization, the book-object seems destined to save a programmatic individuality in the isolated universe of its various perfections.

Lia Drei's book-object *Iperipotenusa* ["Hyperhypotenuse"] features a number of unique characteristics, including a series of die-cut geometric shapes that creates a reading path equivalent to that of the word through the use of differently colored pages, whose fruition appears both "mechanical" and rigorously optical. No disruptive element is to be found within the volume and its complex, concentrated play of elementary signals. According to Giulia Niccolai, the perceived effect is similar to that of the sema-phore flag signaling system.

---

* Udo Kultermann, *Vita e Arte* ["Life and Art"] (Milan: Görlich, 1972).

VI. *From Silence to Movement*

Thus a visual and public literature can only be based upon a type
of "open," global communication that implies all forms of fruition,
from assimilating reading to the deciphering of structures intrinsic
and extrinsic to the text. Yet this procedure does not bring about a
decrease in the semantic value of language, as can be easily verified if we consider that the presence of this value remains constant
and permanent in even the smallest particle of a language, and is
observable as soon as the reader makes use of his experience and
knowledge of spoken or written reality. The goal of the book as a
privileged vehicle of poetic communication is taken for granted
by the majority of those who work in the field of total poetry. Thus
Antonio Porta speaks of his *visual epigrams* as "a practical attempt
to render poetry readable even beyond the customary space of the
book page." And, according to Balestrini, it is the "flight" from
the book that characterizes the new research: "Once the rhythmic
continuum enacted by verse through the book page is broken,
poetry adopts an entirely different metrics, the visual organization
of verbal material in a single two-dimensional space." This basic
theme is linked to Schwitters' idea of the painting-poem, emphasizing its material moment, i.e. pondering the substantial modifica-
tion of the relationship between work and user that occurs when
the latter, longer arranging the printed text in a private or "intimate"
manner, is constrained to evaluate its aesthetic and linguistic
meaning with an immediacy previously unthinkable. In effect, the
physical distance between the text and the reader corresponds to a
tension established between the visual and semantic poles of interpretation. This physical distance between the text and the reader
thus becomes relevant to the aims of an appropriate fruition of the
painting-poem, which is no longer thinkable as only a product of a

verbal operation, but must be considered the result of an interaction between the work and its surroundings.

So, for example, the work of Christian Tobas moves in a post-Dadaist atmosphere toward a linguistic dimension in which the presence of the word almost always coincides with an objectifying semantic purpose, in which visuality is first and foremost the specularity of language, or better yet, of its lexical particularity. Every single word is specifically employed to establish a link with matter, yet that matter coincides with the word by metaphorical or simply tautological means. A painting-poem by Tobas can in effect "recount" the events pertaining to the birth of the word from matter, or vice-versa. As Barilli has written, Tobas does not respect "the normal indifference of signifiers (the audio and graphic part of words) with respect to signifieds or to their conceptual values."

As far as concrete poetry is concerned, the theory of public literature has a nearly absolute value: if Max Bense speaks of advertising slogans, regarding his *Constellations* (1953–1963) Gomringer cites airport signage and street signs. In fact, because of its extreme conciseness the concrete poem can be read instantaneously (much like ENTER or EXIT signs), and it is in this sense that we should understand the passage from verse to the ideogram theorized by the Gruppo Noigandres from 1952.* This passage is based on Ezra Pound's interest for the Chinese ideogram, considered the expression of a mental posture that tends toward maximum economy in the communication of verbal forms. In the *Cantos,* Pound uses the ideogram as a structural principle for the interaction between blocks of ideas that criticize, repeat, and reciprocally illuminate one another, and in so doing, he elevates the relationship between thematic nuclei and graphic space, which becomes an essential factor in founding the body of the poem. According to Hugh Kenner, the Poundian method must be related to Mallarmé's theory of the fragmentation of the idea into allotropic images. In effect,

---

* The *Anthologia Noigandres* (1962) includes the following authors: Augusto De Campos, Haroldo De Campos, José Lino Grünewald, Décio Pignatari, Ronaldo Azeredo. Moreover, the Brazilian concrete poets who head the group's magazine, *Invenção* ["Invention"] are much more numerous; let us mention Luís Ângelo Pinto, Edgar Braga, Pedro Xisto.

with *Un coup de dés* ["A Throw of The Dice"] (1897), Mallarmé
anticipates many of the fundamental solutions of total poetry. By
intensifying the movement of the text with a variety of typefaces,
and distributing groups of words at different points on the page,
Mallarmé transforms the poem into a visual game that is organized typographically in a new spatial dimension, with results that
Valéry would have rightly defined using the "ideographic spectacle"
formula.

With the recent text *Un coup de dés, moins le hasard* ["A Throw of
The Dice, Minus Chance"], Plinio Filho transforms the symbol of
a die into a hexagon, and then a circle, schematically postulating
the passage from what we can define as Mallarmé's probabilistic
hypothesis to a situation of equivalent possibilities and random
circularity, viewed as a repetition of ever identical information
from which the cancellation of creative research in poetry seems
to derive. Evidently, Julien Blaine is also referring to Mallarmé
when, in *WM Quinzième*, he speaks of a seed created by *hasard*
which produces intuitive line-fragments from those designated as
word-forming letters "during the voyage." According to Garnier,
textual meaning in the *Coup de dés* is progressively distanced from
semantics and becomes exclusively formal, i.e. no longer "translatable" but only "transmittable." To be translatable language must
in fact be presented as allegorical; it must be itself and simultaneously something different, that only codified similarities are able to
bring into existence. Instead, in Mallarmé the spatial/typographical
game is an "intimate correlation between poetry and the universe,"
and the text tends to free itself from the semantic incrustations
of words. In this way spatialism annuls the translation code in
order to obtain those individualistic tensions necessary to save the
linguistic values put into a state of crisis by the "language-chatter"
that makes up the background noise produced by mass media. The
abandonment of meaning constitutes a true and actual "mutation"
with respect to preexisting types of communication.

But perhaps the most interesting aspect of Mallarmé's text is in
the clear critical consciousness that accompanies and sustains it. In
the poem's introduction Mallarmé speaks of the assumed importance of the *white space* (which "versification requires as silence")

and the "prismatic subdivisions of the idea" linked to a principal of "simultaneous vision of the page." Even the Futurist notion of simultaneity can be linked to Mallarmé: their "words-in-freedom" constitute the first conscious, explicit rejection of traditional typographic design, and the recomposition of language in a visual form free from rules. With Futurism, there is an evolution from the typically literary concept of poetry to a more open concept tied to the world and its quotidian reality: as Belloli says, this is the transformation of poetry from *song* to *message*. In this sense, Mallarmé can be considered the inventor of a compositional procedure in poetry whose meaning is comparable, according to Augusto de Campos, to Schönberg's "tone rows." Through the research of the historical avant-garde, Mallarmé's postulates, much like those of Christian Morgenstern, Apollinaire, or Arno Holz, lead directly to contemporary experimental poetry; likewise, through the mediation of Anton Webern and others, the notion of "tone rows" is tied to the music of a Boulez or a Stockausen, and thus to an audio universe that endeavors to mend the deep fracture existing between man and scientific reality. It is worth noting that in 1953, following several experiments in linguistic montage, Augusto de Campos achieved the first systematic work of Brazilian concrete poetry (*Poetamenos* ["Poetminus"]) drawing his inspiration from Webern's *Klangfarbenmelodie* ["tone-color-melody"]. It is an extremely important example of a score-poem in which, following the indications of Webern's piece, Augusto de Campos marks the various phonetic timbres by attributing different colors to words, syllables, and letters; moreover, this poem would be vocalized two years later in São Paulo by a group of avant-garde musicians. The principal aspect of this type of poetic creation is the structure of the text: with the term "structure" the Brazilian concrete poets returned to Gestalt psychology, indicating an entity in which everything is more than the sum of its parts, or something qualitatively different from the whole of the elements that compose it; as in Ronaldo Azeredo's poem "Velocidade" ["Velocity"] (1957):

```
V V V V V V V V V
V V V V V V V V E
V V V V V V V E L
V V V V V V V E L O
V V V V V V E L O C
V V V V V E L O C I
V V V V E L O C I D
V V V E L O C I D A
V V E L O C I D A D
V E L O C I D A D E
```

Here Azeredo bases the optical effect on the typographic form
of the letter *V,* and on the vertical, horizontal, and diagonal repetition of this letter. The rectangle is thus divided into two triangles,
one of which is abstract, while in the other the word "velocidade"
is composed or decomposed, according to the direction of reading,
from top to bottom or vice-versa. It is easy to observe that the
poem's graphic layout does not exhaust its aesthetic meaning,
which can only be accurately grasped by identifying the semiotic
and semantic moment. From this point of view, the poem is the
structure and the structure is the poem. This unity does not eliminate creative tension, however: "Every authentic poem," writes
Décio Pignatari, "is a premeditated adventure." According to Max
Bense, a concrete text "identifies its unique linguistic world with
its exterior linguistic world": in fact, the intrinsic meaning of the
words (with their morphemes and their networks) is reflected in
visual adaptation and vocal reproduction.

Concrete poetry is thus presented as the result of a systematic
study of contemporary forms of communication. Its goal is to offer
the reader a text-object that is "useful," "consumable," and that
has nothing to do with the mystagogical reserve of the Romantic,
Symbolist, or Surrealist poet. According to Heissenbüttel, the
Surrealist *poème-objet* has an obvious fetishistic character, and it

only vaguely reconfigures itself into a linguistic relationship that can be articulated. "The objects set side by side here, and to which writing is added with contrasting or labeling effect, function solely as stimuli with regards to the mantic/associative process that unfolds in the observer. The objects thus juxtaposed create an effect of estrangement on the spectator, the reaction they aim to produce leads back to a pre-linguistic state, neither intellectually deducible nor able to be put into words." If instead the poem is structure, structure is reality: the concrete poet works with rigor, like a worker erecting a wall; and, Pignatari adds, his will to *construct* is superior to his will to *express*, or to *express himself*.

In any case we can say that between the terms *poem* and *object* there is a hypothetical distance that should occasionally be verified experimentally, not in the world of logical categories implied by models. For Giulia Niccolai (*Poema & Oggetto* ["Poem & Object"], 1974), for example, the poem is the most hidden sense of the object, its aspiration toward lightness and uselessness. Accustomed to the instrument-object, we are still perplexed before this liberation, this flight of the instrument-object from itself, the horror that the object begins to have of itself as an instrument. The extraction of the instrument from the object has something vaguely surgical about it; the object is no longer an object but not yet a poem, and no one knows if it will succeed in becoming one.

The distance between these two hypotheses is troubling to those who have to verify it, even more so to those who have to annul it, and then there is always the repercussion of reality: if the instrument wishes to remain an instrument once detached from the object, where does it belong? How is it made to survive? The poem prefers to ignore this problem; with or without the object it *exists*. Even if it exists only mentally, no one can negate that existence, and the more its model is suspended in the void the more shines with its own light. But the question that Wittgenstein can ask us is this: does the object know it is no longer connected to the instrument? And what of the problem of knowing whether the instrument has understood it is finished? It is no accident that we are speaking not of the poem-object but of poem and object; missing from this two-sided definition is the idea of paralysis/stupefaction immediately recognizable in the Surrealist *poème-objet* and which is useful for its historical positioning. The refusal of the instrument-object was likely present even in Surrealism, but while the Surrealists decapitated the object to make it dream, we are now witnessing an attempt to make it change places in the series of referential codes. On the other hand, the problem that Wittgenstein could propose to us is no longer valid if it is true that "the connection between the meaning of the words 'they play chess' and the rules of the game is in the list of rules of the game, in the instruction of the game of chess, or in the daily practice of the game," that is, if it is true (or relatively true) that the poem expects to become an object at least with the same *necessity* as that with which the object moves or evolves toward the poem; the meaning of the word "poem" and the meaning of the word "object" are truly connected through the rules of daily practice. Meanwhile, the poem and the object are also fixed on the page or canvas because between all moments of temporal flux in which the two-sided ambiguity presents itself as possible, one side is inevitably privileged, "unique," the one in which in the eye of the observer gathers an unexpected nexus among the discontinuous elements in a series of referential codes. This nexus (that is the "&" of poem & object) is obviously tautological and thus presents itself in response to an expectation; and the response claims to be documented insofar as it is tautological. The expectation, however, is the expectation of the object, no longer an instrument, to be recognized as an element of a duality, not a unity.

Let us now compare Azeredo's poem with one bearing the same title ("Velocidade," 1963) by the Portuguese experimental poet António Ramos Rosa:

```
a   manha   a   moeda   crespa
o   princípio   duma   torre   o   peito   rude

um   boi   na   estrada
os   pés   as   maos   um   tronco   a   ponte
o   corpo   a   terra
a   mulher   atravessada   a   raiva
da   parede   a   sombra   o   peito
o   corpo
```

It is obvious that António Ramos Rosa's compositional process differs radically from Azeredo's synthetic/ideogrammatic method. In effect, this poem develops the idea of velocity by listing words/ things and words/concepts within the linear structure of traditional verse, which is nonetheless interrupted by the spaces between one lexical element and another. Every space functions as a pause, and invites a reading that can mime the fleeting presence of units of landscape closer in relation to the background, represented by the white of the page. In this case, velocity becomes a pretext for expressing in an impressionistic manner, and with an evident play of light and shadow, real or mental, the human condition in the "modern" world. Regarding this text, E.M. De Melo e Castro speaks of a "phenomenological perception of the world." A. Ramos Rosa relates it to the Futurist non-syntax of words-in-freedom, from which it differs only in its more uniform typographical treatment. This fragment of "Uomo + vallata + montagna" ["Man + Valley + Mountain"] (1914) by Umberto Boccioni serves as an example:

```
Echi              dondolio di alberi
     acciottolio              sparire
     entrare procedere nel buco
montagna              ventre buio
rotolio interno              segnali rossi
     metodici              binari
vene              brontolio interno
     uragano lontano              geologica im-
mobilità              trapassa rapidità
     300 cervelli al buio              attesa
     LUCE              vallata              sole
avvicinarsi  avvicinarsi  avvicinarsi
```

On the other hand, and logically so, even in certain Futurist examples the word "velocity" is presented as a particularly mean- ingful model for semantic layout: thus in Franceso Cangiullo's poem "Fumatori" ["Smokers"] (1914), it is composed of characters that become progressively smaller as they approach an imagi- nary horizon. This is a graphic solution typical of the historical avant-garde, and above all of Futurism. On closer consideration, however, there are few words that permit a visual solution so effectively faithful to the meaning, so much so in fact that this solution already comprises a hint kinetic poetry. Kinetic poetry utilizes movement to provoke a controlled transformation or deformation of words, and in so doing, goes beyond the confines of the surface, and enters a spatial dimension. Unlike in kinetic painting, the space created here will be more semantic than visual strictly speaking; the poet substitutes a lexical mechanism for the repetition of geometric forms, and the inevitable semantic implications often end up provoking "expressive" effects that are far from precise. The problem is in assigning importance to the plastic features of the text so that the words are not read and under-stood automatically, but materialize beneath our eyes. There are two ways to resolve such a problem: the first is based on retinal stimuli, and the second requires a real kineticism. Stephen Bann's texts are typical of the first method; letters that form the words are arranged on the page according to optic/perceptive models that accompany or increase meaning. In the second method, there are poetic objects in motion (whether random or programmed) whose abandonment of the page often signifies the abandonment of every established semantic reference or, as in the case of John Furnival, the reformulation of these semantic references according to the probabilities offered by the immobility of the object understood as the initial stage of a kinetic process that is possible but not necessary.

Writing in 1965, Frank Popper maintained that literature was behind the plastic arts, at least regarding a certain number of formal problems: in particular, the possibility of applying the formal and aesthetic patterns of kinetic art to poetry would be inter-esting in the sense that, in the field of literary expression, there is a dearth of efforts to introduce "real movement"; it is better to linger on the notion of "virtual movement" in a way that places the stress on the "primordial" and "necessary" term *movement,* also because many concrete poets (if we want to avoid the definition of op poetry) or spatialist poets have chosen this direction. De Melo e Castro's *Obiecto poemático de efeito progressivo* ["Poematic Object of Progressive Effect"] (1962) is a kinetic book-poem in which the dimensions of the page increase in time with the lexical and visual intensification of the text, constructing in turn a progression from the linearity of the first verse to the spatiality of the last page, according to a rhythm based on meaning. From the initial word, "filula," which is the scar that remains on the branch when a leaf is plucked, begin a series of physiological and naturalist references reduced to the essential, shattered, or playing with various visual compositional techniques. Within the structure of the book-poem, semantic data, caught up in the appearance of a barely hinted at cosmogony, gradually assumes a dense magical/ritual aura.

    fala
    prata

            cala
            ouro

                    cara
                    prata

                            coroa
                            ouro

                                      fala
                                      cala

                            para

                  prata   **ouro**
                  cala   **fala**

                                          clara

Haroldo de Campos, "Concrete Text"

VII. *From "Constellation" to Negative Black*

The synthetic/ideogrammatic method of the Brazilian concrete
poets was born of a rejection of free-verse which, according to
Haroldo de Campos, after *Un coup de dés* is only an "alibi." If on
the one hand Mallarmé proposed the organization of graphic space
as a natural force field for the poem, on the other the research of
Pound, Joyce, and Cummings pushed the linguistic possibilities of
the literary text beyond all limits. In particular, the practice of visual
atomization that Cummings exercised on verbal material irrefut-
ably demonstrates the inanity of any process inherent in free verse.
As, for example, in the following poem (1940):

                    !blac
                    k
                    agains
                    t

                    (whi)

                    the sky
                    ?t
                    rees whic
                    h fr

                    om droppe
                    d

                    ,
                    le
                    af
                    a: ;go

                    e
                    s wh
                    lrll
                    n

                    .g

The Brazilian concrete poem is set in the sphere of this dialectic of form, of this "qualitative evolution," and explicitly assumes responsibility for a *living tradition*, particularly since it rejects every solipsistic conception of art. In this way, the Gruppo Noigandres also goes back to the specifically national tradition, referring chiefly to the poetry of Oswald de Andrade (1890–1954), one of the principle exponents of Brazilian literary modernism, which was inspired by Italian Futurism. From the poetry of Oswald de Andrade – characterized by an absolute lack of rhetorical elements and an extreme epigrammatic rarefaction of the text – a path leads through the work of poets like Carlos Drummond de Andrade and Murilo Mendes up to the compositions of João Cabral de Melo Neto, in which a taste for stripped-down versification laid out within a Neoplastic form predominates. Oswald de Andrade intended Brazilian poetry to become a "product for export," and thus put an end to the age-old South American cultural dependence on Europe. Clearly, as we have seen, concrete poetry was born simultaneously in Brazil and Europe,* in the sense that it is a similar, if not identical approach to the relationship between literary creation and sociological reality. In both cases, the poem is seen in its materiality as an instrument that interprets the world according to an aesthetic methodology that takes the typical procedures of mass media into account.

Haroldo de Campos says: "Concrete poetry speaks the language of today's man. It rejects the craftsmanship, discursiveness, and metaphor that transform the poetry of our age – marked by technological progress and non-verbal communication – into an anachronism that causes the divide between poet and public often deplored in sentimental terms that are anything but objective." From this perspective, the synthetic/ideogrammatic method that brings all textual elements (audio, visual, semantic) into play can be considered an organizational process of the poem in exact consonance with our civilization's need for as rapid and direct a message as possible.

---

* Actually, in the case of Carlo Belloli we may speak of a "pre-concrete" poetry, from the moment his first texts of this kind appeared in 1943.

sem um numero
 um numero
  numero
   zero
    um

     o

      nu
       mero
        numero
         um numero
          um sem numero

Augusto de Campos, "Concrete Text"

The same comments are valid for Eugen Gomringer's *constellation*, understood as "the simplest visual model of poetry constructed with words," and which is immediately manageable in its totality as well as in its individual parts. Gomringer starts from the realization of the increasingly radical formal simplification of our languages: "Often the content of a phrase is translated into a word-notion and differing explanations are concentrated in small groups of words. The demand to substitute plurilingualism with a few commonly used languages is also notable." This tendency toward a reduced and essential language from which superficial national characteristics progressively vanish is not necessarily disconnected from the aims of poetry. "Concentration and simplicity," writes Gomringer, "are the soul of poetry." Instead, we are witnessing the implementation of a problematic that invests both poetry and language with the same intensity. Both proceed toward a schematization that is functional with respect to the requirements of instantaneously "readable" information. Moreover, concrete poetry, that possesses structures of immediate visual apperception and relatively pure signage, adapts quite well to functioning as a link between different kinds of language, or between different national languages. Hence the possibility that concrete poetry may realize the idea of a universal poetry, that is not only "international," but "supranational." According to Gomringer, this conception of poetry is closely tied to the condition of the poet in today's society. One cannot speak of art for art's sake because concrete poetry, which establishes a valid level of communication for all intents and purposes, lives in symbiosis with reality: "The question of content presents itself to the concrete poet as something strictly linked to a precise way of living for which even art has a rational function. Its behavior is positive, synthetic/ rationalist. So are his poems, which do not serve to convey any kind of sentiment and thought, but consist of plastic spaces of language in close contact with modern tasks of communication based on the natural sciences and sociology. To the concrete poet, a given content can be interesting only if its spiritual and material structures can be elaborated in a linguistic structure." Here is a *constellation:*

> ping pong
> ping pong ping
> pong ping pong
> ping pong

Above all, the *constellation* is born of the need to not go beyond the word, whose "average common sense" is preserved, toyed with, or "constrained" according to the boundaries imposed by rationality. If for Gomringer concrete poetry is also an "adherence to content" (but content is interesting "if and in that its spiritual and material structure can be elaborated in a linguistic structure"), this insistence on the word effectively acknowledges the refusal of all forms of contamination that are non-*ascetic*, that is neither "concentration" nor "simplification" with respect to various possible and ultimately desirable extra-linguistic contributions. Gomringer initially proposes to influence at least everyday language with "the new poem," an aim that can only be achieved by imposing the text on the "movement of language." However, that movement has a privileged relationship with elements that belong almost exclusively to the "external" typographic world, and in which the poet's "ludic talent" must intervene and take control. And this ludic talent does indeed trigger the exact mechanism of the *constellation,* although this interpretive suggestion of the work is only implied by Gomringer, and stands more as a comparison to the idea of the concrete poet as "seeker of new formulas," rather than as a technician "of the rules of the game and of language."

According to Arrigo Lora-Totino, the visual poem (and this term is used in reference to overcoming concretism as proposed by Belloli) cannot be limited to being a useful object. That is because the concept of the functional aesthetic object is currently in a state of crisis and must be replaced by a "disciplinary principal of the integrative organization" of the values in play, and not only verbal, plastic, or audio values, but also elements of a finalized research into "inhabitable" spaces. These spaces correspond to the needs of a civilization that is not only technologically developed but also "highly structured." In *Arguments,* Ulises Carrion adopts the typical visual surface of concrete poetry, but rigorously limits the lexical material to people's names. But to speak of limitations is erroneous since the series of nouns seems inexhaustible to the reader, based as it is on a vast number of combinations and graphic solutions. A new universe unfolds before our inclination to designate a person with a word that is simultaneously "his" and anyone else's who might wish to adopt it for him or herself. Thus the relationship between designator and designated enters a state of crisis for the semantic ubiquity of *Mary, John, John & Mary,* whose simple listing assumes the disconcerting form of a challenge to meaning. The visualization contributes to this effect, introducing elementary designs often used with irony and ambiguity, especially if we consider such visualization relative to the concept of "calling," in the double-sense of "to give a name to" and "refer to" someone (and thus "functionality" is in crisis).

There are practically no differences between Gomringer's synthetic/rational method and the synthetic/ideogrammatic method of the Gruppo Noigandres. However, the *constellation* is based on the linear distribution of elements and extremely rigorous compositional control, while the texts of the Brazilian concrete poets are often characterized by a multi-dimensional ordering of signs within the space of the page, with results that evoke a type of "visual Baroque." As in this poem by José Lino Grünewald (1959), for example:

```
       f o r m a
     r e f o r m a
   d i s f o r m a
t r a n s f o r m a
   c o n f o r m a
     i n f o r m a
       f o r m a
```

This tensional diversity at the moment of composition can
be explained by differing cultural influences. As we have already
noted, the "living tradition" of the Noigandres includes – other than
Brazilian Modernism – a vast zone of experiences from Mallarmé
to the Joyce of *Finnegans Wake*, through Pound, Tzara, Apollinaire,
Marinetti, and Mayakovsky. On the other hand, Gomringer's points
of reference are the De Stijl movement[*] and the Bauhaus, but
especially the Swiss school of post-World War II graphic design,
concrete painting (Max Bill) and Arno Holz (*Phantasus*, 1898).

In fact, Arno Holz's serial writing represents the first systematic
attempt to resolve the contradictions inherent in Symbolist-type
poetic language, which oscillates chaotically between the phonetic/
visual dimension and that of content. In *Phantasus*, Arno Holz
breaks verbal material into three serial forms that intertwine in
various directions and that periodically embody simultaneous positions. Words are coordinated according to semantic analogies (and
concepts referring to the same field of meaning are then grouped
together), according to grammatical function (adjectives, participles,
nouns, etc.), and according to phonetic values (words of analogous sounds). Here, says Gomringer, "the material and technical
categories dictate the construction of the work." For Max Bense,
Phantasus is an example of statistical style, in which the text's
aesthetic realization stands in relation to the frequency with which
individual textual events are verified, like the number of syllables
in a word, the number of words in a proposition, the degree of

---

[*] In the second De Stijl Manifesto (1920), signed by Theo van Doesburg, Piet
Mondrian, and Anthony Kok, we read: "The word is dead. The word is
impotent... The word must be reconstructed to follow sound, ideas... For the
modern writer, form ought to have a direct spiritual meaning."

mixture ("textual entropy") between words with different numbers of syllables, and so on. Arno Holz renders poetically valid words of five, six, seven syllables, as well as those with an even greater number of syllables ("kokosfasermattenbelegt"), thus introducing random textual events with a high degree of improbability.

By the end of the nineteenth century, the problem of a new poetic language had already taken root and been configured more or less with today's connotations. On the one hand, to the semantic movement we must correlate an analogous visual/typographic movement that exalts the meaning of poetic composition by increasing the levels of reading, exploiting however only the traditional space of the page. On the other hand, the premise for a phonetically-driven use of poetic composition has been posed, and can already be roughly understood as a musical score. An interesting attempt at fusing the double-edged sound/figure problematic in the score-poem was made by Christian Morgenstern in his 1905 *Galgenlieder* ["Gallows' Songs"], the best known of which is undoubtedly the "Nocturnal Song of the Fish." As Carlo Belloli wrote, "the text promotes a concrete idea of integration with the visual without turning to the semiotic/typographic or calligraphic translation of its semantic structure." In fact, in "Nocturnal Song of the Fish" Morgenstern restricts himself to replacing the verses with their corresponding quantitative metric scheme (*short* and *long*), creating an essential model for positioning the time element within the space element, thus obtaining a perfectly visualized image of silence.

Christian Morgenstern, "Nocturnal Song of the Fish"

As we can see, the problem is no longer only that of giving a typographic/spatial dimension to verbal material, according to Mallarmé's suggestions. Morgenstern's score-poem opens new perspectives, casting doubt on the survival of the word as a poetic instrument by definition. If aphasia is one solution, today it is being suggested by many poets: Heinz Gappmayr, for example, invites the reader to "guess at" or "think of" a poem behind a black screen, a geometric smudge that covers the imaginary (or real) preexisting text; Mary Ellen Solt's "Moonshot Sonnet" simply reproduces the pattern of frame lines used in photographing the moon ("I noticed," writes Solt, "that by simply copying these symbols, I could make a visual sonnet. No one has been able to write a sonnet to the moon from the Renaissance on, and I could not do it unless I was willing to incorporate its new scientific content. The sonnet was a supranational, supralingual form like the concrete poem. "Moonshot Sonnet" is both a spoof of old forms and a statement

Mary Ellen Solt, "Moonshot Sonnet"

about the necessity for new ones."); Öyvind Fahlström utilizes an endless variety of symbols, then repeats them in circular compositions like letters of a non-existent alphabet. In Václav Havel's *Alienation* he adopts the orthographic sign of the "period" to designate an ironic and absurd map of the labyrinth in which we live; some of Julien Blaine's texts were created by repeatedly pressing a thumb tack smudged with ink onto the paper; Jan Burka, in his anything-but-random *Homage to Christian Morgenstern*, invents a series of cryptograms positioned to imitate traditional versification, thus playing with the poem on two levels that appear mutually incompatible at first glance. This inclination toward a non-verbal poem can be explained by the need felt by many poets to establish the various components of total poetry in the most elementary fashion possible, and return to pictography and ideography. The Lettrists' calligraphic creations, or certain Dadaist-type texts like Man Ray's "Lautgedicht" (1924) are all connected to the same

Man Ray, "Lautgedicht" ["Soundpoem"]

tradition. With this "sound poem," Man Ray does not stop at making his profound diffidence to all types of writing visually explicit, but by pushing Morgenstern's intuition to the limits, he offers us a "non-text" obtained by erasure. Being a score-poem, "Lautgedicht" serves as a model not only for poets like Franz Mon or Emilio Isgrò, who at times "write" by erasing words in a preexisting text, but also for musicians like Giuseppe Chiari who, in *Beethoven* for example, uses the same procedure on a classical score.

In *Prix Nobel* ["Nobel Prize"] (1960), Reuterswärd implodes arguments about the abolition of the word by abolishing even the letters of the alphabet and by using punctuation marks exclusively. Given the insistence on quotation marks that characterizes it, this volume (about one-hundred pages) becomes an inimitably cold satire of spoken language, just as the pauses in the notation of a musical score highlight the parallel lines of the staff. After all, this insistence on quotation marks distinguishes the procedure from a simple neo-Dadaist retort against the pretext of semantic habits. We are thus presented with a manual on the ideology of silence, which is reinforced by the fact that the book is devoid of critical comment by the author, as well as of any type of editorial presentation. An object among objects, punctuation responds only to itself, avoiding the microcosm of the letter that begins to appear far more vast and "comprehensible" than Lettrist hypotheses might make us suppose. In this way Reuterswärd works toward a further miniaturization of this microcosm, taking it to the threshold of annulment, without however renouncing the idea of writing, whose visualization usually only constitutes its corollary. In fact, that which can be read between the punctuation marks is not at all identifiable with blank space, since it is semantically altered by the reflection of the punctuation marks themselves.

A "non-text" can also be made by superimposition: Bob Cobbing prints a poem on the same page repeatedly, making it roll or moving it up and down in such a way that the different printings never coincide. At a certain point, a central zone becomes very heavy and practically illegible since it is almost completely inked, and doubled, tripled, etc., lines emerge. Some words are still recognizable, though the interweaving of contrasting angulations makes reading particularly difficult and ambiguous. The semantic disintegration and graphic compacting of the verbal material occur simultaneously, and the informal availability of the rigidly geometric features of the page is born of this incongruity.

The following statement by Franci Zagoričnik concerns the foundation of the very notion of literature: "All literature is negative. Its most fortunate meaning is that it is meaningless." In the case of Zagoričnik, poetics and the literary text are interchangeable, one could even say that only this disposition to a substantial identity of the two moments guarantees the survival of poetic discourse. If we consider the *Scripta* texts, by far the most exemplary part of Zagoričnik's research, we have no trouble realizing that here the "negative" or "meaningless" use of the typewriter's keyboard ("the writer writes: in order to do so, paper and 'pen,' or better yet 'typewriter' suffice") is related to the techniques of optical art, and is thus a "pure" use, or at least one contrary to verbal operation. The charismatic power inherent in the destiny of the poet understood as the transporter or inventor of a message, a communicational pattern, is resolutely refused by Zagoričnik: "Literature is not in correspondence with the world because correspondence or colloquia with the world are not possible. Many things are a fine 'know nothing.' (...) Literature (...) speaks a language that man barely understands, or that actually escapes him."

Franci Zagoričnik, "Coexistence"

In Michele Perfetti's *Point poème* ["No Poem Period"], the thesis of the annulment of writing begins with a well-devised rhetorical artifice: a circle a few centimeters in diameter is used as a lens to be applied to preexisting material, and the "content" of the circle is modified in various passages, from the still syntactic sentence to a clausal chunk deprived of meaning, from the word to syllabic presence, from photographic image to absolute black. The poem can be a "negation of the text" for Ferdnando Millán as well: the written part which forms a geometric shape is juxtaposed with a black square of the same dimensions indicating its cancellation or annulment, whereas white would indicate only its absence.

In the poem *Fouilles anticipées* ["Anticipated Excavations"], Bory uses negative black with allegorical intent, the birth and death of the Earth are phenomena depicted through the formation and destruction of words around a circular smudge of ink: the allegory is simple, when the words are legible an idea of the world (that is language) exists, but when the words are swallowed by the dark-ness, the reader is presented with a total linguistic void, that is, with the disappearance of reality. The hypothesis is that the "antici-pated excavations" can provide some indications as to the legibility or rather the existence of data concerning an essential, "literal" cosmogony. The round smudge (black and negative) remains at the center of the action unfolding on the page: here the kinetics requires about twenty pages to be demonstrated, like a series of slides projected on a white screen at identical intervals notwith-standing the diversity of the photograms' semantic presence. The use of a kinetic allegorization displaces the effects of visual poetry into a complex terrain, where offering a sequence of linguistic events means placing one's trust in the repetition/modification of an image composed of words, that is, of a sentence being formed identical to the one a reader "sees" by turning the pages. All of this corresponds to the idea of a book that explores "a space that is always open and always closed, page by page: the preceding pages dead, the following pages yet to be born."

In Maurizio Nannucci's *chromatic poems,* many of concretism's characteristic elements give way to a uniform use of color whose tautological presence (red corresponds to the word "red," yellow corresponds to the word "yellow," etc.) is not meant to heighten the semantic values of the text, but rather to attenuate if not actually abolish its meaning. The typewritten text consists of schematized repetitions of the word indicating the color printed in the color indicated on a page of the same color. The play on words is inevitable here and, on closer inspection, it is here that we find the meaning of the message: the chromatic uniformity seems to suffocate every other possible interpretation, the repeated assertion is similar (but not identical) to the self-negation on the visual plane. Thus the absence of lexical variations corresponds perfectly to monochromy, and the word "red" becomes only a "brush stroke" of red added to the preceding layers: in this way it suggests a more ambiguous variant of the practice of annulled poetry. This type of research is taken farther by Nannucci with the *definitions,* which constitute a true tautological corpus, and tautological "by definition," relating to an obvious series of "quoted quotations" and "indicated indications" (and naturally the list is presented as never-ending). These the author extracts from the language understood not only as Saussure did, as the "sum of deposited imprints on every brain," or as "the sum of verbal images imagined in every individual," but also as the alibi of non-communication between subject and object, where the object is simply disguised by a repeated predicate, and thus self-annulled. It is a form of cold delirium whose first point of reference, conceptual art, is placed between parentheses – an "internal" operation that does not seem to predict or auger any solutions. We can say that Nannucci proposes a tautological art, or an art of impoverished tautology, by placing parentheses around conceptual art now understood as a "probably" false balance between subject (art) and that which ultimately reveals itself to be a repetitive predicate (conceptual) – which then is the most direct way to negate space and "halos" of meaning. Evidently, the definitive procedure also becomes a non-procedure, an absence of reaction to the concept. For us this absence seems to be predicted by the notion of tautology but which in this case serves rather to cast doubt on tautology itself at the moment in which it is presented as irreversible, a definite definition, a tautological tautology.

As for Claudio Parmiggiani, his "illiterate" writing is not, by definition, far removed from Kolár's hypothesis on the possibility of reducing written language to a system of signs *independent* of alphabetization. At the same time, it utilizes a different form of visual presence, in which there is a strong intervention of graphic elements that can be placed in relation to an abstract logology presented as *dependent* on forms of writing already perfectly organized at the beginnings of prehistory. Since Parmiggiani often uses the term "papyrus" (and also seeks to recreate it as an object), it is easy to think of one of his versions of hieroglyphics in terms that can obviously not be connected to any morpheme. The negation of every semantic reality, however, makes the "papyrus" (or the "scribe") assume a fetishistic role, a role in which the visualization of the text *is* the text. Though the text can have a meaning (lost, or to be found) ad absurdum, the fetishization of the object "papyrus" or of the object "scribe" cannot not coincide with the photographic image of it that is being presented, since even writing is only the specularity of the sign itself from the moment it renounces being read in order to read itself.

neroneroneroneroneroneroneroneroneroneroneroneronero
neroneroneroneroneroneroneroneroneroneroneroneronero
neroneroneroneroneroneroneroneroneroneroneroneroncnero
neroneroneroneroneroneroneroneroneroneroneroneronero
neroneroneroneroneroneroneroneroneroneroneroneronero
neroneroneroneroneroneroneroneroneroneroneroneronero
neroneroneroneroneroneroneroneroneroneroneroneronero
neroneroneroneroneroneroneroneroneroneroneroneronero
neroneroneroneroneroneroneroneroneroneroneroneronero
neroneroneroneroneroneroneroneroneroneroneroneronero
neroneroneroneroneroneroneroneroneroneroneroneronero
nercneroneroneroneroneroneroneroneroneroneroneronero
neroneroneroneroneroneroneroneroneroneroneroneronero
neroneroneroneroneroneroneroneroneroneroneroneronero
neroneroneroneroneroneroneroneroneroneroneroneronero
neroneroneroneroneroneroneroneroneroneroneroneronero
neroneroneroneroneroneroneroneroneroneroneroneronero
neroneroneroneroneroneroneroneroneroneroneroneronero
neroneroneroneroneroneroneroneroneroneroneroneronero
neroneroneroneroneroneroneroneroneroneroneroneronero
neroneroneroneroneroneroneroneroneroneroneroneronero
neroneroneroneroneroneroneroneroneroneroneroneronero
neroneroneroneroneroneroneroneroneroneroneroneronero
neroneroneroneroneroneroneroneroneroneroneroneronero
neroneroneroneroneroneroneroneroneroneroneroneronero
neroneroneroneroneroneroneroneroneroneroneroneronero
neroneroneroneroneroneroneroneroneroneroneroneronero

VIII. *From "Surface" Text to "Extensive Collage"*

On the other hand, albeit with different results, in his desire to deny legibility Mon often adopts the technique of décollage (or its opposite though complimentary technique, collage) in his work. In fact, in many of Mon's poems of this type, the forms resulting from the random or geometric cutting of verbal material have a double dimension (positive and negative), and the meaning of the text is derived from the integration of letter fragments and white spaces.

Franz Mon, "Collage-Text"

In Mon's intentions, the play of empty and filled spaces must lead to a "surface" poetry that tends to painting, in that writing was formerly pictorial in nature and probably expressed much more than spoken language. Thus the poem must rediscover the visual qualities that were lost when printing, which standardized writing, reduced it to a mere function of sound. "This language," writes Mon, "is only for the eye, even if it presupposes spoken language and its use." A compositional method analogous to Mon's was followed by Fernando López Vera and Ignacio Gómez de Liaño. Both of these Spanish poets push the text toward a pure abstraction that no longer has any semantic relation to the initial verbal material. Certain poems by the highly prolific Kolár are born of an attitude of this type. But Kolár's collages are always so perfect in their balance of schematization and randomness that it is difficult to pinpoint the real matrix of the extraordinarily difficult and rarefied optical effects that he obtains. Even I used the collage technique in the *zeroglyphics,* applying it to advertising texts that, in order to verify the thesis of Max Bense, I considered "projects" of concrete poetry. In these poems, the word or phrase that I used is often recognizable despite its deformation or simplification. In his poem *lyrik,* Franco Verdi works in a similar fashion, rendering its meaning even more explicit by introducing clearly understandable lexical elements. From this point of view, both *lyrik* and certain of my *zeroglyphics* make one think of Kriwet's *poem-painting* more than of Mon.

Unlike the concrete poetry of the Gruppo Noigandres or that of Gomringer, which communicate their own structures, these texts (collages or décollages) establish an emotional relationship with the reader. They are perceptible instantaneously, but not rationally. Luigi Ferro's *iconigrammi* ["iconograms"] or certain poems by Emilio Villa, for example, fix fragments of printing types in alternative resettings whose legibility is produced by the play of unpredictable visual correspondences. And it is precisely the unpredictability of the message that is the most salient characteristic of this kind of poetry. The text's degree of asemanticity takes on a fundamental role here. The farther it withdraws from the rules of daily language, the more the concrete collage-poem invents a personalized reading code. This somehow seems to retrace in reverse the road opened by concrete poetry toward a supranational and objective linguistic reality. But this is a false impression. The concrete collage-poem

Adriano Spatola, "Zeroglyph"

tends to revalorize the subjective impulse, but not to refute the idea of a universal language. Rather, it participates in its creation precisely because it revalues the pure imagination, detached from any reference to the immediate cultural and linguistic fabric.

In *Corriente alterna* ["Alternating Current"] (1975), José Antonio Cáceres – member of the Gruppo N.O. of Madrid, founded in 1968 to conduct research into concrete and experimental poetry – proposes to explore a zone of signs supposedly situated beneath the threshold of perception: a world of symbols soon to be destroyed or deprived of meaning, even if their simple presence would make one imagine the existence of a "visible" reality through them. This effect is obtained through the use of broken, eroded, and illegible transfer type set against incongruous directional elements, semblances of scores, shadows of nonsensical mechanisms corresponding (as the title of the book suggests) to a certain ironic tone with regards to Futurism.

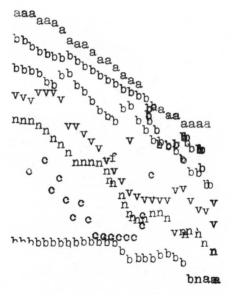

J. García Sánchez, "Typed Poem"

On closer inspection, the manner in which these poets deal with typographic material as a point of departure is identical to that of the *bricoleur*. The poet today faces a reality that is already "written," a world covered with signs, and poetry by now consists almost entirely of the utilization of this limitless repertory to aesthetic ends. The poem by the Spanish poet Ocarte, in which you can see a man bombarded by letters and writing, makes for an efficient if simplified image of this situation. In *Entropico* ["Entropic"] (1966), Vaccari exclusively adopts verbal material from newspapers, conserving it unaltered or emphasizing its graphic features, with a procedure that recalls Balestrini's *cronogrammi* ["chronograms"]. Unlike Balestrini, however, Vaccari also incorporates figurative elements that serve as pop counterpoints within a logical/ alogical discourse that interpolate pre-existing messages in ironic fashion. Moreover, while Balestrini's *cronogrammi* are constructed through the superimposition and intersection of linguistic fragments leaning toward a chaotic, absurd semanticity (that, among others, recalls Portuguese poet António Aragão's *poesia encontrada* ["encountered poetry"]), Vaccari's poems often indulge in word play with a didactic flavor. In both cases, poetry is put forward as a destructive criticism of mass media and naturally of the culture that it implies.

Nanni Balestrini, "Chronogram"

According to Giuliani, this attitude could derive not only from "linguistic impatience," but also from the "pleasure of mistreating the newspapers and their habit of momentarily rationalizing the tragic, the vain, the incontrollable, the filthy, and the pathetic, in their headlines and columns." Visual poems would thus be produced as a response to "the exquisitely schizophrenic incongruity" of the combinations caused by an arbitrary reading of the news and commentaries. "By pushing our will to the limit," writes Giuliani, "it is possible to extort a reflux of meanings or non-meanings from fragments cut out then glued together in powerful nuclear suggestions, so that the (experimental) disarticulation and rearticulation of the text reveals certain structural constants of our linguistic world." Here the adverb "exquisitely" – one cannot help but notice – obviously recalls the *exquisite corpses* of the Surrealists, who sought the principle character of poetry in the "invention" or "rediscovery" of a schizophrenic language. Moreover, in this case we are dealing with an absolutely unknown moment with respect to Surrealism, which today can be correctly interpreted and judged only in light of the use that mass culture was able to or wanted to make of it. Carlo Munari writes: "Surrealism, having invested every creative activity, had to condition advertising to a significant degree. And advertising, to the extent that it is an expression necessarily related to an average collective taste, had to demonstrate in turn the vast spread of Surrealism. Today, perhaps, visual habit impedes us from fully evaluating the revolutionary changes that occurred in advertising during the 1920s, and the influence that Surrealism exercised in the following decades, right up to the present day... But there is more: the typical linguistic ingredients of Surrealist art, if conveniently adapted and emptied of their excessive qualities (sadism and demonology) – have proven to be extremely effective to advertisers for psychological persuasion. The shock the Surrealists aimed for proved to be profitable for market propaganda." This adaptation to the average collective taste is considered by some a "betrayal" of Surrealism; from the point of view of the new poetry, which refuses to position itself at a remove from reality, it can only be profoundly meaningful. The interest in the ideological options of the historical avant-garde must not in fact be separated from an analogous interest in its collapse. If the mercantile prostitution of the artistic product was so blatant and violent in Surrealism, it is obviously due to the fact that perhaps more than any other movement, Surrealism endured and often provoked all of the typical ambiguities of the relationship between art and bourgeois society, just as it provoked and endured the typical ambiguities of the relationship between art and Marxist ideology. In a word, Surrealism sought to push to the limits the eternal facts of a tragic and grotesque impasse, that of an apparently dead-end alternative between "a (bourgeois) literary career and a (Marxist) revolutionary career," as André Breton has written. It thus becomes possible, if one thinks of what is said of Rimbaud, to speak of a revolutionary shamanic function for the poet, as opposed to the standardized, conservative shamanic function performed by the technological elites.

This point brings up another of the essential components of total poetry: *engagement*. Naturally, this is not the traditional notion of "commitment" that is still tied to discursive and sentimental poetry, and not only in Europe. This type of committed poetry does little more than overindulge in nineteenth-century petit-bourgeois formulas, not only in style, but in its entire attitude toward reality. It is a dead poetry, and is only kept alive for "political" reasons. But it is certainly not for the sake of contradiction that its survival can be described as the fruit of a misunderstanding, and that, all things considered, the strictly "political" results of this poetry were rather pitiful. So now is still the time to put this word on trial, and to cease blindly defending it out of a workplace obligation. Today, the state of the notion of commitment is that of a building conserved in façade only. Like the label of a sealed but empty jar, it is now only useful to cheat consumers. Moreover, it is an absolutely vague notion used nevertheless with the same conscientiousness and pedantry as an precise scientific instrument. The fact is that for some time now it has ceased exercising any active force, and is content with pure and simple reflexive action. It is so reduced that it fails to question any vision of the world, and it develops along the lines of current opinion, inviting the reader to resignation. But the only "commitment" possible is that of fighting resignation.

If we consider the ambiguity of the word *engagement*, we must admit that the term "participation" used by Brazilian concrete poets is more appropriate (and less ambiguous) to designate this tendency of total poetry. In Brazil, the "participation" of concrete poetry in sociological and political problematics is linked to both João Cabral de Melo Neto – who in the poem *The River* (1954) offers us a lucid testimonial on the dramatic condition in the Nordeste without forsaking the rigor of his compositional method – as well as to the example of Mayakovsky. "Without revolutionary form, there is no revolutionary art," the latter asserted, and it is from this critical perspective that we must consider the thesis of the "semantic concretization of composition" formulated in 1961 by Décio Pignatari. The refusal of cultural dependence on Europe that we mentioned above has already been transformed into explicit and violent scorn for the "American way of life" in the following poem by Pignatari (1957):

```
b  e  b  a      c  o  c  a      c  o  l  a
b  a  b  e                      c  o  l  a
b  e  b  a      c  o  c  a
b  a  b  e      c  o  l  a      c  a  c  o
c  a  c  o
c  o  l  a
                c   l   o   a   c   a
```

In Haroldo de Campos' book-poem *Servidão de passagem* ["Transient Servitude"], the contrast between the commonplaces of poetic language and the facts of a desperate social reality take on a tone of ferocious refusal: "blue is pure? blue is pus ... green is alive? green is a virus." In *Estele Cubana* ["Cuban Stele"] (1962) Décio Pignatari constructs a text filled with anger by utilizing a variety of characters and artfully shattered words. And in *Revolução* ["Revolution"] (1961), José Lino Grünewald uses a lean, cutting, political vocabulary. In the following text, Grünewald, transforming the noun *fome* (hunger) in the verb *come* (eat!), composes an epigram of notable effect:

```
f o m e
f o m    e
f o    m e
f    o m e
  c  o m e
```

In a word, according to Haroldo de Campos, next to the avant-garde of "ontological solitude," tied to nihilism and solipsism as discussed by Lukács, there is room for a constructive and "participatory" avant-garde, the avant-garde of Mayakovsky and the extremely synthetic poetry of Bertolt Brecht. It is within this sphere that Brazilian concrete poetry would like to be situated.

After all, the ideological option does not belong to the Gruppo Noigandres alone. In many texts by the American Jonathan Williams, for example, we find a similar attitude, filled with merciless irony, as in the poem "*A Mnemonic Wall Paper Pattern for Southern Two-Seaters,* based on the obsessive repetition of *black only* and *white only*. With *r = revoluzione* ["r = revolution"] and other such texts, I hoped to create a series of political slogans made of a single word and dedicated to May 1968. On the same argument, in *Mai 1968: Manifeste sous forme d'idéogrammes* ["May 1968: Manifesto in the Form of Ideograms"], Julien Blaine made a leaflet in which the contrast between revolt and power is visualized through a use of an extremely simple, but highly efficient symbology.[*] But, more than in concrete poetry (or semiotic poetry, in Blaine's case), it is in visual poetry that political discourse can be realized by critically manipulating the alienating images that constitute the *leitmotif* of consumer culture. In Italy, it was first and foremost the Gruppo 70 that furthered this discussion, consistently running the risk of falling into the old type of *engagement* that we have already criticized. And we must admit that this risk is not easily eliminated, since the visual poetry of the Gruppo 70 tends to overturn messages of mass communication and thus contest a phenomenon that presupposes and fuels the passivity of those receiving the information, and in this process it is easy and often necessary to

---

[*] Blaine's technique owes much to that used by El Lissitzky in his poster *Beat the Whites with the Red Wedge* (1919).

imitate the sub-aesthetic values of kitsch, if only to negate them. According to Filiberto Menna, "visual poetry is born of the poet's intent to not avoid the clash with the outside world but, on the contrary, to operate within the same mass culture, attempting an aesthetic promotion of the banal, of the quotidian, and of kitsch." To this end Pignotti speaks explicitly of "counter-advertising," "counter-comics," "counter-glossies," defining visual poetry as "the gesture of those who return the merchandise to the sender."

This "gesture" recalls Giuliani's attitude of repudiating news-papers. But Giuliani's visual texts push verbal material into the dimension of the absurd and the grotesque, while the poets of the Gruppo 70 tend toward the creation of a shared semantic value that is not divorced from current language. In fact, the latter replace Giuliani's "linguistic impatience" with a form of "linguistic patience," so to speak, accepting to engage mass media on its own terms, that is by turning, at least potentially, to the same public. "If the public does not look for poetry," writes Pignotti, "poetry must look for the public." The first step to take in working toward such an objective is naturally that of taking poetry from the place where it has always been hidden – the book – and making it available to an unlimited number of "readers." And we must also continue to replace the word with the image, which is more responsive to the needs of immediate, direct communication, and more in tune with the reality in which we live, dominated as it is by what Dorfles calls "artificial images" (posters, television, cinema, etc.). Also poetry, like art, "tends to flee the places it is usually collected and is in search of new spaces, different publics, or of differently placed perspectives with respect to the urban scene," as G.B. Nazzaro has said. For Pignotti, poetry *can* become a means of mass communica-tion, and is similar to an advertising slogan that has already been coined but has not yet been put in circulation. The passage from word to image cannot be brought to a conclusion, because visual poetry needs to use the word to "comment on" or "explain" the image, with the aim of not losing any opportunity for ideological contact with the public. While in concrete poetry the word itself is constructed as an image, in visual poetry a true interaction between the two is indispensable, and it is from this interaction that what

A. Russo defines as "the image/word amalgam" is born. Thus, according to Pignotti, "visual poetry is not founded on a linear and temporal reading of semantically separate verbal and iconic elements, but on a simultaneous, total, relational reading: the whole prevails over its constituent parts." The visual text is thus a global text that, for Michele Perfetti, moves toward a desecration of the usual expressive order.

In any case, a visual poem is always a collage-poem, and the visual poet, like Franz Mon and other concrete poets that work in this direction, is above all a *bricoleur* in that he collects verbal and non-verbal materials that originate in a preexisting written reality. But we are dealing with two different, even opposed types of *bricolage*. "The autonomous universe of language defines the limits within which the concrete poet operates; there is no place for extra-linguistic elements, as there is in visual poetry," says Arrigo Lora-Totino. The concrete collage-poem tends toward a certain asemanticity and abstract design, while the visual often delves into caption-like effects based on the play of estrangement resulting from the combination of elements drawn from non-homogenous contexts. In this case, according to Miccini, we are dealing with an extra-textual poetry that is entirely lost in the body of the appropriated discourse, which has been "physically" modified in order to change the passive stance of the reader of the source text, a text that originally lacked the ironic (or satiric) component which in the end becomes rather obvious. To underline the difference between the visual collage-poem and any other form of collage, Pignotti speaks of *extensive collage*, thus emphasizing the extension and complexity of the linguistic and figurative material used.

The notion of *extensive collage* draws on that of a *technological poetry*, and that is a poetry "written in today's and everyone's language," whose roots extend into the extra-literary terrain of mass communication. A "second vocabulary" emerges from this terrain. It is made of chunks of prefabricated language, functional to the needs of industrial reality, but also susceptible to aesthetic transformation. The technological collage-poem uses verbal or visual stylemes from the public domain, but as we have seen, it does so with a destructive will. Thus, says Luciano Ori, the visual poet escapes the urgency of consumerism and the "bombardment" of mass media, and realizes their pragmatic meaning: poetry transforms the chronicle into history, and that which is art "in a nutshell" into art. "Not one intervention, unless it be random, of subjective experiences... they are replaced by the apersonal choice of available technological material. The conclusions are sentimental, emotive, moral, social, etc., and every reader will draw them for himself, according to his own nature and experience, participating in the work that thus becomes an 'open' work. The result should be an epic, objective, almost "Homeric" language, because it is choral."

Let us focus on Luciano Ori's work, specifically on those visual texts he produced between 1963 and today, that is over the course of more than ten years, more or less from the foundation of the Gruppo 70 with Pignotti's relative "technological poetics" to today's diaspora of styles and intentions. Naturally, Ori's discourse cannot be homogeneous; the relationship between his poetry and reality is tied to the tremors of the chronicle, and to a taste (often insipid) for the random and useless. It is not easy to save or somehow essentialize this relational material, nor is it necessary for a poet who can make brutal use of the filter of the grotesque, or the weapon of ideological purpose. Certainly the more recent things, based on the simple reproduction of the comic strip, almost a Lichtenstein in the Italian style, insinuate the suspicion of a decontextualization that is all too elementary, uncritical, and complicit with a passively accepted mass media message.

But the *Concerto caldo* ["Hot Concerto"] and the *Concerto per alberi* ["Concerto for Trees"] represent one of the truly interesting moments of this situation. In the two *scores* notation is replaced by symbolic images that are rigorously allusive to an estranged condition, and the indication of "movements" in its precise ambiguity creates the effects of a visual symphony. Unfortunately, statements like, "visual poetry is a synthesis of an anthropological turning point" and "visual poetry is the proletarian alternative to literary capitalism," are better suited to *épater les bourgeois* (according to an antiquated tradition) than to provide information on possibilities for research.

In visual poetry, according to Achille Bonito-Oliva, the poetic product "is proposed as an 'intentional object' for the existing inter-penetration of form and function." The articulation of connections within the text brings about a new unity whose fundamental char-acteristic is the defeat of the most probable and defining hypothesis of reading. From this point of view, the "strategic behavior" of the poet consists in the construction of an alternative to the institu-tional linguistic system, and the result can be measured by consid-ering the gap between the reacquired mobility of language and its initial automatism. Nevertheless, "compositional procedures must not be made into absolutes, so as to avoid merely copying the technological matrix at the base of the social system." This warning further clarifies the substance of the ideological problematic inter-woven into the visual poetry of the Gruppo 70 and of many other authors, Italian and otherwise, whose work has the same premises but points toward a different relationship or balance between verbal and figurative elements: Jochen Gerz, for example, like Norman O. Mustil or Stelio Maria Martini. But Lucia Marcucci deepens the discussion: "Keeping in mind the technological era in which we move," she writes, "both research and researchers must pass through mass media, that is they must direct all experiments into a sphere of common vehicles of communication and search for a grammar capable of acting on human conscience, of exalting its critical role, and of culturally politicizing the masses." Naturally, it is not possible to pursue such an objective without forsaking in practice, and not only in theoretical formulations, the habitual places for consuming literary products. Visual poetry is often no more than framed poetry, which limits itself to renouncing the book in order to accept the art gallery, and thus to abandon one elite public for another. But like painting, music, or theater, even poetry attempts to break this closed circle in order to seek out and provoke the user in his own environment. For total poetry, it is no longer simply a question of the quality of the procedure, but also, and especially, of the quantity of results, if the optimum result is obtained with the creation of a new type of user, finally liberated from every form of uncritical reception of the message. In short, the new poetry wants to "replace" mass media.

Thus, Marcucci uses the poster as a very public instrument for some of her technological texts, while Ian Hamilton Finlay speaks explicitly of the poster-poem and Ketty La Rocca constructed absurd street signs. Even I, with Landini and Parmiggiani, put together a series of political posters ("posters" in the real sense of the word, since they were actually posted in the streets of Bologna, Modena, and Reggio Emilia in 1964–1965). The fact that they had a political character is important: our intent was to act right where the problematics of communication were most blatantly out of date. And beginning with the refusal of the static/optimistic sphere of the sentimental, using a para-Surrealist model we sought to subvert the institutionalized rules of the ideological/public relationship, through the use of aesthetic categories such as surprise, irony, the grotesque, and bad taste. Fabio Bonzi was exploring this same space with his poster book, which used extremely banal lexical and iconographic material, thus aiming for an ideological shock that the writings, which commented on figurative carry-overs, emphasized at every level of reading. He also hoped to reach a public broader than the usual readers of poetry. But it would be an error to attribute this need to one group, or to a few isolated authors. As we have seen, this must be considered the essential feature of the new poetry, and the shared platform for the most diverse investigations. "The world can be read," says Blaine, "so it is no longer a question of thinking it or translating it, but of restoring it." Thus, in order to create his *plastic poems,* Kitasono Katue rejects every instrument still linked to literature and uses a camera exclusively, because, "the camera can create a poetry of insignificant objects." The presence of words and objects could bring to mind the relation between the plastic poem and the Surrealist-type *poème-objet.* But unlike the Surrealists, Kitasono Katue creates only ephemeral constructions, linked to the specifically Japanese tradition of the "ikebana," in order to photograph them, and it is the photographic image that constitutes the "definitive" plastic poem.

If it is true that the poet and reader can regard reality with the same eyes and act upon it in open collaboration, because to write, according to Max Bense, "means to construct language, not explain it," it is also true, however, that in recent years the old idea of poetry as a political slogan has resurfaced with remarkable persistence, and in certainly more aggressive forms, a visual poetry that seems to impose a certain number of formulas on the reader. The very title of the magazine that has carried out this program, *Lotta poetica* ["Poetic Struggle"], is certainly revealing. Besides, Sarenco, who was the magazine's main promoter, never hesitated in his choice of critical methods based on verbal violence. One of the polemics propagated by *Lotta poetica* (but, above all, at the market level and thus in relation to a problematic that our book can only touch upon) was against conceptual art. To this end Dorfles spoke of a *querelle* between visual/concrete poets and "pure" conceptualists for a question of priority in the exploitation of the verbal element to neotic/visual ends. For Dorfles, it fell to concrete poetry to first use the verbal typographic element for the purpose of visual composition. "While visual poets usually aim to obtain an 'aesthetic' result, one of visual pleasure," we can also note that for the pure conceptualists this result "is usually neglected, or explicitly avoided."[*]

In a critical note on the work of Mirella Bentivoglio, who belongs to this area of research, Renato Barilli has instead distinguished two types of "conceptual": the North American, "mystical/ecstatic conceptual, steeped in Zen spirit, even if it is careful to unfurl in a cold climate"; and that which represents the point of arrival for visual poetry "in which an extremely cultured and 'precious' spirit transpires in the historical sense of this term."

---

[*] G. Dorfles, *Ultime tendenze nell'arte d'oggi* ["Recent Trends in Today's Art"] (Milan: Feltrinelle, 1973).

IX. Solipsism or Behavior?

The magazine *Ana Etcetera* was born in 1958 and (supposedly) died in 1971. Ten issues in a dozen years are sufficient to evaluate the "work in progress" (one of the labels appearing on the cover of the magazine) of a meta-communication that claims to be "virtually private." To avoid any misunderstanding of the role of privacy in the field of experimentation on "abstract philosophy" and language, the general policy of *Ana Etcetera* is also defined as the possibility of "writing in a circle," and of a "communication service."

It is obvious that the primary function of such defining enticements is to confront the reader with a sphere of intervention in which linguistic analysis and self knowledge, philosophical heterodoxy and the individual exercise of thought (even of unthinking), and typo/graphy as a constituent element of discourse and the *sense of sense* are all contemporaneously set in motion. This sphere of intervention is to be considered open to both behavioral rites and interlanguage.

Naturally, for our part, we shall emphasize typo/graphical methodology to verify its distinctive characteristics with respect to similar operations implemented at the same time: as we have seen, *Ana Etcetera* aims for a linguistic analysis, but such an analysis must be "graphic" and thus relative to both the mode of representing words in writing and writing itself understood as "form." The graphic analysis of language, writes Martino Oberto, is "a method of reading as a direct graphic image of the world (for transcription) in the transcription: if it is defined as a problem of 'form,' the question leaves us indifferent – in fact if we are presented with different modes (or forms) of the same thing, it is a pseudo-problem in that we are facing a question of formal indifference – that is the choice of the type of writing is free, arbitrary" (*Ana Etcetera* 6 [1965]). Writing consequently moves into areas of meaning that lie between terminological elements and signs placed at the operator's disposal and used by him for a "disorganized opus." This disorganization is the continuously postponed (at the metalinguistic level) result of research. Here, in my opinion, writing or typo/graphy serves to make the course of research, postulated as infinite, explicit and symbolized according to extremely synthetic conventions.

The defining enticements in question thus also have an internal use, at the very moment in which one accepts the obvious presupposition that the definition coincides with the formation of the concept; this use is not regressive in character, though it does lead to a "solipsistic" writing, a "secret" language (Oberto actually speaks of "autism"). The arbitrariness of the choice of writing technique is kept functioning even as a method of disorganizing information, without limiting the semantic expansion, or rather the semantic charge primed in the metalanguage. And here we can have an explosion, but also an implosion, with writing in search of itself, notwithstanding the warning that for metalanguage one need not understand "a language used to speak of language." This implosion – writing in search of itself – is actually closely related to Wittgenstein's assertion that "That which does not get expressed in the sign is shown by its application. What the signs conceal their application declares." (*Tractus logico-philosophicus,* 3.262). Such an "application" is consistent in *Ana Etcetera,* from the point of view of the graphic analysis of language, based on a "semantography" in which (for particular "conditions of dislevelment") "words get used as signs." It is evident that the discussion does not deal directly with poetry but would rather occur at a level on which the manipulation/symbolization of sign, word, or word-sign triggers a process of coagulation of meanings either dispersed or hidden (dispersed in the world that surrounds the text; hidden between the folds of the text), a process similar to that which Jung calls the "individuation" or the "centralization of the unconscious." In this light the appeal to a secret language seems more plausible, a language that comes into being for the text, especially for the visual text, a collection of formulas to be exploited for the purposes of "writing in a circle," which I find rather obvious in the work of both Anna and Martino Oberto. Perhaps Ballerini is right when, having revealed a "visual expression of logical processes" and a "refusal of the notion of language as mimesis" in this work, he arrives at the assertion that in recent years we are confronted with the "assumption of signs as pre-telepathic convention." However Anna Oberto's most recent position has turned out to be rather independent with respect to the theories of the magazine, based on a "poetry in the feminine" having prioritized ideological connotations with respect to a "language in the masculine." In my opinion, such a priority is configured more in terms of organization than negation: from the simple "feminist manifesto" Oberto moved to "visual narratives" created with her very young son. The sign that the child traces on the page with the pronunciation of a word (his own or one suggested to him) serves as a point of reference for a series of analogical elements whose choice is always the product of a collaboration: to "magic" objects like stones or shells are added photographs, notes, and alphabetic letters. These circumstantial aspects are perhaps less interesting on the visual than on the conceptual level, but regardless, they allow for useful encounters with other "primitive" dimensions of total poetry, and can be considered *hors langage*, as Jacques Lepage would say.

To return to *Ana Etcetera,* on a less abstract/theoretical plane and more related to the text's practical composition, Ugo Carrega's note on the poem "Relationship between the Poet and his Work" (in the magazine's sixth issue) is rather revealing. Here the printed page is no longer considered a "means for multiplying the handwritten page" but an "expressive instrument-in-itself," in so far as "everything laid out on the page is capable of communication." The poet always had to battle the linearity of language, where for linearity we mean that "physicity" that allows us to say only "one thing at a time" and whose sole escape route is the stratification among images, meanings, rhythms, etc. Next to this *verbal element* of the printed page there is a *graphic element* based on the layout, lettering, and created or carried over signs. While the layout responds to a "desire for clarity" in the arrangement of words in a given space, lettering allows the typographic character to be used semantically.

The created sign "is nothing more than a movement of the hand on the page to stabilize its trace, its physical/emotive presence, or its 'dazzling thought' in the dimension of its easy, rapid acquisition." As for the carried over sign, it is "all that material of pre-existing printed paper chosen by cutting up and inserting into the text as a carry-over of an objective reality."

These annotations can be interesting since they significantly simplify the poetics of *Ana Etcetera,* so much so in fact that they reveal a certain number of suggestions that seem to conflict with the idea of a solipsistic writing. Besides the pedagogical intonation (the layout as a desire for clarity, and "also out of moral obligation"), Carrega certainly has a very different attitude toward objective reality and its carried over signs than that intuited in Oberto's proclaimed autism, where for autism we literally understand the tendency for thought or perception to be regulated by personal desires or needs rather than by objective reality.

However, this difference is in great part annulled by the importance that Carrega gives to the created sign (for which the definition "creative" sign might be better). On the other hand, in a diachronic verification of poetics we could say that the refusal of linear language and its consequent stratification is as related to certain fundamental Futurist suggestions as the appeal to "dazzling" thought is. But such a hypothesis, though ostentatiously confirmed by the example used for its lettering (*terrrOOReeee!*), remains a hypothesis in principle only, since the sensitivity in the handling of verbal material is simply too different in the two cases. Rather, let us say that Carrega did not limit himself to re-evaluating a tension within the visual text that Futurism was able to exploit according to a linguistic code *separate* from a material code. Instead he uses a pluridimensional intensity that implies the existence of semantic surpluses attributable to (or deducible from) every element of the world in which we live, and in which written or spoken language obviously represents only one of the many means of communication.

In *Segni in uso* ["Signs in Use"] (defined as "verbal exercises") Carrega wonders how in a book "the support," in other words the page and paper, can *not* be "semantically employed," which

tàs! tàs! tàs! tàs! tàs!

unvrienendorstònebal!

Ugo Carrega, "Symbiotic Writing"

presupposes that in every other such case the support necessarily
carries a semantic weight which the poet must take into account
if he does not want to produce a message that is only partially
conscious. In fact the question more specifically concerns that
which occurs when the lack of images or phrases promised by the
captions on certain pages immediately and automatically creates a
range of meanings based solely on the support. Regardless of the
clear contradiction, Carrega insists on the fact that "the constant
diversity of the signified" depends "on the constant diversity of the
signifier," but in this context what are we to do with the blank space
on the page? Are visual/semantic and averbal space not the same
thing? It is interesting to note that *Signs in Use* is resolved with a
few false syllogisms, like:

> walking is a gesture
> walking is a sign
> the gesture is a sign
> the sign is an object
> walking is an object.

And here, naturally, no one can intervene as to the validity of this sophism, which the author could always describe as concerning a process of progressive objectification of learning mechanisms relative to experience. The "verbal exercises" thus claim to become indemonstrable statements whose apparently logical reasoning actually utilizes the physical support to confuse appearance with substance. The text can be indifferently present or absent, insofar as its visuality does not depend on this presence or absence. Regarding Carrega, Aldo Rossi writes: "I believe it has been demonstrated that between *seeing* and *reading* (an image, but also *writing*) the former action is necessarily primary: it follows that at first glance writing (handwritten or printed) is taken in as an image framed in a precisely delimited space (the page)." *Signs in Use* pushes this premise to the limits, taking this assumption for granted, especially in the series of "un-realizable pictures" in which reference to the image eliminates the image itself and takes its place.

We can better understand this process through the concept of *symbiosis,* on which the magazine *Tool* (1965–1967) based its research. *Tool* was born of a "serialized" program that in each issue presented a given type of relationship between the various elements of graphic poetry. "Symbiotic writing" should be understood as an interlanguage in which signs taken from different languages participate equally, in the scope of an analysis of the printed page. Such analyses focus primarily on visual particularities that can be reutilized for purposes of communication that is no longer *physical,* as for example in Futurism or concrete poetry, but *abstract* (that is, logical or artificial).

The parallel with *Ana Etcetera* is obvious, even if *Tool* proposed an essentially autonomous discourse on the possibility of a "logical lyric" as the point of departure for a way of working within poetry that is virtually exclusive and limited to a pre-established nucleus of experiences. Thus in symbiotic writing three "readings" are involved: the first "ostensive graphic," the second "ostensive phonetic," and the third "semantic verbal," however without it being necessary to adopt the idea of simultaneity.

Lino Matti, "Symbiotic Text"

It is true that the simultaneity of the three readings leads to a "maximum of poetic communication," but it is equally true that a certain dispersion toward secondary directions branching from the primary three brings the poet to a personalization of the *poiein*, in an "attitude" of "absolute freedom of ideological action," all the more so since *tool* means *instrument* and that "the use of an instrument alters he who uses it and the necessity of speaking of the instrument he wants to use."

Aside from the not entirely acceptable considerations on the exclusion of concrete poetry from the models of artificial communication, or on the identification of Futurism with a model of physical communication (and we have focused on this argument more than once), the magazine has without a doubt thoroughly researched the six elements that constitute symbiotic writing: its phonetic aspects, propositional statements, lettering, sign, form, and color. Still in the scope of *Tool*, the poetry of Vincenzo Accame comprises a series of variants, a closed series that is nevertheless justified as open and almost infinite in that it plays on the literal role of the variant.

Vincenzo Accame, "Symbiotic Text"

Language, or rather its visual reading, springs from this balance and defers from page to page (and pages are syntactic decisions) the repetition of a few words used, objectively, as interpretive keys for the commentary the book makes on itself as a system of signs, but also, and perhaps most importantly, from within, as conventionally abstract elements that can be imbued with semantic values. This convention is identical to that which makes musical logic a metaphysical texture (it is certainly not by chance that Accame refers to the technique of the "variation"), and it is thus the problem of constructing a text independent of

its meanings. According to Tomaso Kemeny, Accame's intent is
to stage verbal and graphic material in "support-space" in order
to make the operation itself coincide with its derivative meaning,
abolishing the historical/metaphysical points of reference external
to the support-space that is thus "made active" to the point of
"declaiming" its presence. That is why Accame's text remains on
this side of communication, in the normal sense of the word, and
of expression: "the connotative function of language, its paradig-
matic dimension is reduced to zero" and "through the regression of
meaning to its origins, gesture becomes frozen at the threshold of
writing."

Ben Vautier, "Postcard"

At a certain point, visual writing techniques exploded and
rejected the discussion of the process of textual formation, moving
toward the problem of a behavioral poetry. The moment of this
explosion must be situated at the beginning of the '70s, if we
decline to consider the preceding phenomena of absolute negation
at the intermedia level, the most clamorous and acceptable of
which is that of Ben Vautier (I say "acceptable" from the point of

view of research on total poetry). But the unknown quantity of this passage to behavioral poetry consists of the fact that it reflects via appropriation an analogous system of gestural expression already found within poetry. It is the typical relationship of "parallel" generalization reversed, within the genre, in the destruction/ reinvention of an autonomous model. By now however we recognize that these passages from one genre to the next re-enter a praxis accepted and even invoked by the very life of artistic media. The new way of producing poetry through behavior can only be explained by recalling a broad background in which the individual exploits of this or that "precursor" count less than the effective formation – at the aesthetic level – of a space of creative global freedom.

If, on the other hand, visual poetry is considered as a chain of functional montage in itself and thus with respect to the ideological system of existing cultural relationships, the logical result is that its renewal seems possible only on the political plane, or at least by privileging the "open" relationship with the public, politically speaking. But one must ascertain whether this functionality within the system is real, and not just a simple polemical expedient. For example, Luigi Ballerini's thesis is that visual poetry has acted and continues to act as a disalienating force, that is, against "groups in power" that profit from the "age-old process of standardizing the imaginative" resulting from the act of "fixing" verbal language into neutral printed pieces of writing, in codes repeatable to the point of being worn out, and that the individual cannot instill with anything personal." Thus visual writing, Ballerini affirms, "postulates a recu- peration of the id, not at the level of its most immediately vitalistic requests but inasmuch as it is presented as the total storehouse of perceptive possibilities, provoking a reinsertion of such possibili- ties into the processes of capturing the real."

Ballerini's thesis is satisfying because it bases on the liberation of the id not so much a series of visual texts (belonging more- over to various "schools") as the very procedure for producing them. Thus a rather precise idea of behavior is already contained in visual writing, and we would do well to keep this in mind so as to not burn all bridges behind us in order to move behavioral poetry forward. After all, two examples of *body poetry*, like Claudio Parmeggiani's *scriba* ["scribe"] and Timm Ulrich's *Fig. 1,* use the body as page, not as gestural machine, thus rebalancing the data of the problem. Ferrò's *Dada* is situated on the same plane, but with a very interesting variant from the point of view we are discussing: to graphically render his *body poem* meaningful, Ferrò is constrained to "go backward," that is to use the page-object, with hole-punches and such, while Parmiggiani and Ulrichs settle for the photographic medium. One of my texts, "voyage," exists in two versions that mutually integrate and explain one another, much like the object-poem and the gestural poem. Alain Arias-Mission, one of the most important authors of behavioral poetry, went from happening to public action and then into photo-collage, using the latter to recapitulate and "fix" prior experiences in a new bewildering version. We could easily continue the list of variations on the theme of behavioral poetry's difficult autonomy with respect to visual writing.

Another question worth considering is how the problematic of behavioral poetry does not always have an outright "political" meaning. It has or has had one in certain cases, for example in that of Julien Blaine and his posters (*Regardez la révolution en marche* ["Watch the Revolution in Action"]) pasted on moving objects, such as cars or other vehicles, to make the slogan "effective" and "visible" on the level of the real, with an obviousness that is only tautological at first sight. It does not or has not had one in certain other cases, or unless we noticeably alter the adjective "political," or water it down in a specious way. Behavioral poetry is also an end in itself; it is "useless" and lacks "positive" implications. It can be collective, but can also be developed as an individual moment of an objective situation or even as a moment of subjective, private tension (we are clearly returning to Ballerini's thesis on the recuperation of the id), without however falling into solipsism, without the subject of the behavior being constrained to not admit an external reality different from the fantastic projections of thought or the imagination.

For example, Vaccari's *Per un trattamento completo* ["For A Full Treatment"] is a type of catalogue in the form of a souvenir from a trip recollected and relived through receipts from Diurni Cobianchi hotels, well known to travelers in need of a quick shower or shave. From this point of view, what we have here is a homespun *Odyssey*, the chronicle of an emigration from province to province filled with boredom and routine. In such cases, it is "life" that is called into question, with its tasteless, submissive *mise en scène*.

Franco Vaccari is a fine interpreter of this non-catastrophic fatalism, and for many years he has focused primarily on the trivial and occasionally Grand Guignolesque traces of the "subterranean" implication of daily life. This attitude or "behavior," which has not been steeped in messianic waters, is not inclined to crepuscular melancholy, and allows *For a Full Treatment* to speak only of itself, with the cold logic of supermarket pricing, without the critical intervention or destructive will of the author. With regards to the second way of reading the book – as a "travel-poem" or "action-poem" – I would say that this results directly from the lexicon of receipts, which is offered up to a philological interpretation that is perhaps an ironic attempt at a *jeu de mots*: "aesthetic supplement" for example. Those fortuitous metaphors that bite at reality according to the logic of chance, superfluous texts whose innocent and practical truth has already been absolved *before,* in the limbo of good intentions, and good intentions are impracticable not only for "life" but also for "art" or "poetry."

At the end of all this, Julien Blaine proposes "colon open quote" poetry, an attempt to regroup visual poets around a formula generic enough to remain untouched by the polemics among the various factions. It is in essence a formula of expectation, and the graphic sign itself used to indicate the movement (a colon between quotes, ":") has more the meaning of a company trademark than of an *ism*. On the other hand, Blaine's operation is affected by at least two conditionings: on the one hand the crisis of '68, on the other, the end of that attitude of active collaboration between different personalities differently creative that inspired *Approches* and in part, at least initially, other magazines. Therefore we have a decisive conversion to anonymity and to the dialectical method, as well as to the will to act on daily life within "a given society at a given moment." "Colon open quote" poetry is materialist, and refuses the reading of the *récit* ["narrative"], the fraud of the book, the mercantilism of the object, the alienation of the spectacle. But above all, it refuses to have *language* as its subject, in that its subject is criticism, the multiplication and proliferation of *languages*. The magazine *Doc(k)s* was born of this attitude, and for now is entrusted with new international and total poetic research.

El Lissitzky, "Beat the Whites with the Red Wedge"

Giulia Niccolai, "Poem & Object"

Jiří Kolár, "The Apple"

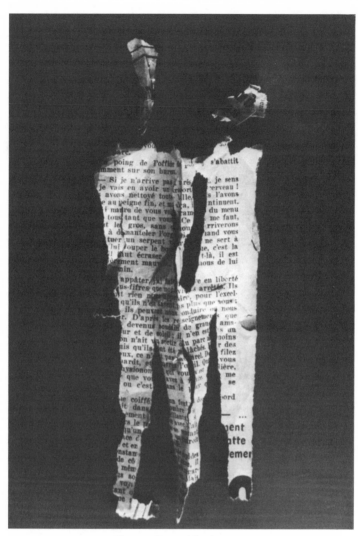

Kitasono Katue, "Plastic Poem"

Eugenio Miccini, "Visual Poem"

Lamberto Pignotti, "Visual Poem"

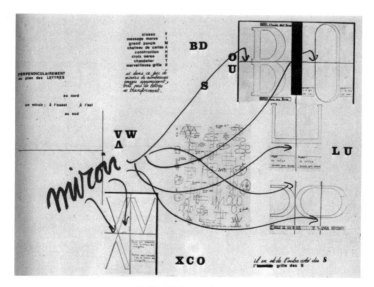

Julien Blaine, "Mirror"

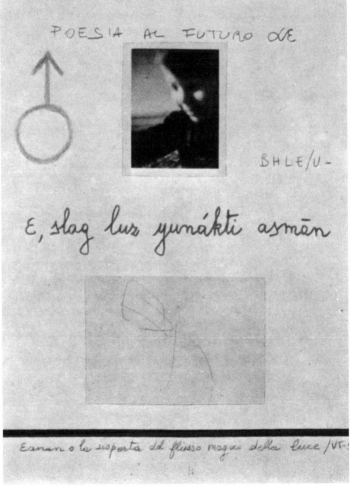

Anna Oberto, "Text Created in Collaboration with My Son"

Carlo A. Sitta, "The Enigma of Isidore Isou"

Rolando Mignani, "Symbiotic Text"

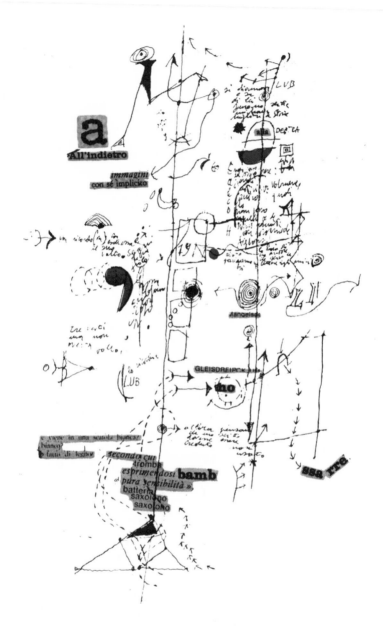

Magdalo Mussio, "Writing"

Martino Oberto, "Ana"

Fernando Millán, "Visual Poem"

Lucia Marcucci, "Visual Poem"

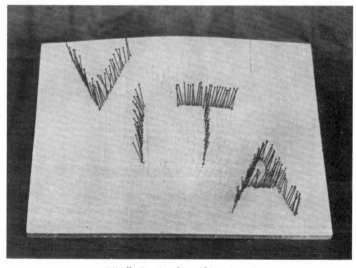

Mirella Bentivoglio, "Object-Poem"

Jean-François Bory, "Visual Sculpture"

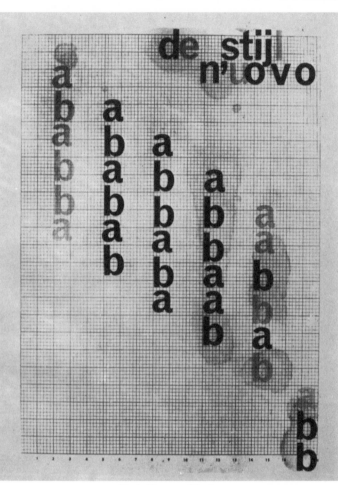

Mario Diacono, "Text"

Stelio M. Martini, "Visual Text"

Bibliography*

ANTHOLOGIES

Aragão, António, and Herberto Helder. *Poesia experimental.* Lisboa: Edicões de autor, 1964.

Azeredo, Ronaldo, Haroldo de Campos, José Lino Grünewald and Décio Pignatari, eds. *Antologia Noigandres.* São Paulo: Massao Ohno Editora, 1962.

Bann, Stephen, ed. *Concrete Poetry.* London: London Magazine Editions, 1967.

Bense, Max and Elisabeth Walther, eds. "Konkrete poesie international." *Rot* 21 (1965).

———, eds. "Konkrete poesie international 2." *Rot* 41 (1970).

Blaine, Julien and J. F. Bory, eds. "L'érotisme dans la poésie matérielle." *Approches* 2 (1966).

Blaine, Julien, ed. "La poésie hors du livre hors du spectacle hors de l'objet." *Robho* 5/6 (1971).

———, ed. "Poésies et expressions d'avant-garde en Amérique Latine." *Doc(k)s* 1/2/3/4 (1976).

Bory, J. F., ed. *Once Again.* New York: New Directions Publishing Corporation, 1968.

Boso, Felipe and Ignacio Gómez de Lima, eds. "Experimentelle dichtung in Spanien." *Akzente* 4 (1972).

Bowler, Berjouhi, ed. *The Word as Image.* London: Studio Vista, 1970.

Brecht, George. *CcV TRE: Fluxus Magazine : New York 1964–1970 (9 Issues).* Milano, Italia: Flash Art, 1970s.

Caruso, Luciano and Stelio M. Martini, eds. *Tavole parolibere futuriste (1912–1944).* Naples: Liguori, 1974.

Caruso, Luciano and Corrado Piancastelli, eds. "Il gesto poetico." *Uomini e idee* 188 (1969).

Caruso, Luciano and Giovanni Polara, eds. *"Iuvenilia loeti", raccolta di poeti latini medievali.* Rome: Lerici, 1969.

---

* [*When possible, we have indicated English editions of works Spatola cited in Italian translation.*]

Chaleil, Andre and Max Chaleil, eds. "La poésie après le verbe." In *La Créativité en noir et blanc*. Paris: Nouvelle éditions polaires 1973.

Dencker, Klaus Peter, ed. *Text-bilden, visuelle poesie international*. Cologne: DuMont, 1972.

de Palchi, Alfredo and Sonia Raiziss, eds. "New Italian Writing." *Chelsea Review* 18/19.

de Rook, G. J., ed. *Historische anthologie visuele poezie*. Brussels: Rijkscentrum Hoger Kunstonderwijs, 1976.

de Vree, Paul, ed. "Konkrete poezie." *De Tafelronde* nn. 2/3, 1966.

Gomringer, Eugen, ed. "Kleine anthologie konkreter poesie." *Spirale* 8 (1961).

Donat, Branimir and Vera Horvat-Pintarie, eds. "Oslikovljena rijel'; Konkretna poezija." *Bit International* 5/6 (1969).

Grögerová, Bohumila and Josef Hiršal, eds. *Experimentalni poezie*. Prague: Odeon, 1967.

———, eds. *Slovo, pismo, akza, hlas*. Prague: Odeon, 1967.

Groh, Klaus, ed. "Visuell-konkret international." *Und* 11/12 (1973).

Hallain, Marc and Others, eds. *La créativité en noir et blanc*. Paris: Nouvelles Editions Polaires, 1973.

Kistler, Horst, and Karl Heinz Roth. *Die Sonde: Zeitschrift für Kunst und Versuch*. 1964.

Lora-Totino, Arrigo, ed. "Poesia concreta." *Modulo* 1 (1966).

Lora-Totino, Arrigo and Adriano Spatola, eds. "Situazione della poesia concreta." *La Battana* 12 (1967).

Luca, Mario Persico, Stelio M. Martini, and Enrico Bugli. *Linea sud. nuova rassegna d'arte e cultura d'avanguardia Anno II-n. 2*. Napoli: Luca, 1965.

Mac Low, Jackson and La Monte Young, eds. *An Anthology*. New York: 1963.

Miccini, Eugenio, ed. *Archivio di poesia visiva*. Florence: Techne, 1970.

———. *Poesia e/o poesia. Situazione della poesia visiva italiana*. Brescia-Firenze: SARMIC, 1972.

Millán, Fernando and Jesus García Sánchez, eds. *La escritura en libertad*. Madrid: Alianza Editorial, 1975.

Mon, Franz and Manfred de la Motte, eds. *Movers*. Wiesbaden: Limes Verlag, 1960.

Morandini, Giuliana, ed. "Poesia visuale, poesia concreta." *Carte Segrete* 20 (1972).

Nannucci, Maurizio, ed. *Exempla*. Florence: 1970.

Pignotti, Lamberto, ed. *Poesia visiva*. Bologna: Sampietro, 1965.

Plamen, I. G., and Marko Pogaćnik. *Eva*. Kranj: Samozaložba (vsak avtor je izdajatelj svojega dela), 1966.

Poésie en question. Opus international, 40/41. Paris: Georges Fall, 1973.

Ruhm, Gerhard, ed. *Die wiener Gruppe.* Hamburg: Rowohlt, 1967.

Schmidt, Siegfried J. *Konkrete dichtung: Texte und Theorien.* Munich: Bayerischer Schulbuch-Verlag, 1972.

Shimizu, Toshihiko, ed. "Experiments in Visual Poetry." *Mizue* 6 (1975).

Solt, Mary Ellen, ed. *Concrete Poetry.* Bloomington, Indiana: Indiana University Press, 1968.

Spatola, Adriano, ed. "Antologia di poesia concreta." *Il peso del concreto.* Ed. Ezio Gribaudo. Turin: Edizioni d'Arte Fratelli Pozzo, 1968.

Spatola, Maurizio, ed. *Geiger.* Turin: 1967–77.

Todorović, Miroljub, ed. "Konkretna, vizuelna i signalistilka poezija." *Delo* n. 3. Beograd, 1975.

Tomić, Biljana, ed. "Poesia visiva in Jugoslávia." *La Battana* 22/23 (1970).

Vergine, Lea, ed. *Dall'informale alla body art.* Turin: Studio Forma, 1976.

Vree, Paul de. *Poëzie in fusie.* Bladen voor de poëzie, 16. jaarg., Nr. 6–8. Lier: De bladen voor de poëzie, 1968.

Wildman, Eugene, ed. *Anthology of Concretism.* Chicago: Swallow Press, 1967.

Williams, Emmett, ed. *An Anthology of Concrete Poetry.* New York: Something Else Press, 1967.

Znamenja, Ljubljana, 1969.

CATALOGS

Accame, Vincenzo, and Friedrich W. Heckmanns. *Visuelle Poesie.* 1969.

Ballerini, Luigi, ed. *Italian Visual Poetry.* New York: Finch College Museum, Instituto italiano di cultura, 1973.

———, ed. *Scrittura visuale in Italia.* Turin: Galleria Civica d'Arte Moderna, 1973.

Bentivoglio, Mirella, ed. *Parola immagine oggetto.* Tokyo: Instituto Italiano di Cultura, 1976.

———, ed. *Poesia visiva.* Rome: Studio Artivisive, 1973.

———, ed. *Tra linguaggio e immagine.* Venice: Gallerio It Canale, 1976.

Bentivoglio, Mirella, Giovanna Sandri, and Adriano Spatola. *Poesia visiva 3: "poesia concreta.".* Studio Santandrea, no. 65. Milano: Studio Santandrea, 1977.

Berner, Jeff. *Aktual Art International: Posters, Manifestos, Objects.* Stanford art book, 8. Stanford, Calif: Dept. of Art & Architecture, Stanford University, 1967.

Carrega, Ugo, ed. *Verso una terza dimensione della scrittura.* Genoa: La Bertesca, 1973.

Carrega, Ugo, and Jiří Valoch. *Tool etc: poesia visiva italiana.* Jihlava: Oblastní galerie Vysočiny Jihlava, 1969.

Caruso, Luciano, Eugenio Miccini, and Maurizio Nannucci. *Formato lib(&)
   ro: mostra del libro/oggetto in Italia : Comune di Firenze : Fortezza da
   Basso, Firenze Libro, Firenze, 7/15 gennaio 1978.* S.l: s.n, 1977.
Contemporanea. Rome, 1973. Includes a special section on visual poetry
   edited by Mario Diacono.
Cooperative de Producción Artistica, eds. *Concordancia de Artes.* Madrid,
   1967.
Cox, Kenneth R., and David Verey. *Arlington-Une: Summer '66.* Cirencester,
   England: Printed by Earle & Ludlow, 1966.
Della Casa, Giuliano, Claudio Parmiggiani, and Antonino Titone. *Km
   149000000. [Mostra], Comune di Ferrara, Centro attività visive, Palazzo dei
   Diamanti, 14–30 novembre 1968.* Cento: Siaca – Arti grafiche, 1968.
de Rook, G. J., ed. *Anthologie Visuele Poezie.* Utrecht: Galleria 't Hoogt, 1976.
Fagone, Vittorio, ed. *Raccolta italiana di nuova scrittura.* Milan: Mercato del
   Sale, 1977.
Goeritz, Mathias, ed. *Poesía concreta internacional.* Mexico City: Universidad
   Nacional Autonoma de Mexico, 1966.
Grossi, Pietro, Arrigo Lora-Totino, Lara Vinca Masini, and Enore Zaffiri,
   eds. *Ipotesi linguistiche intersoggettive.* Florence: Centro Proposte, 1966.
Hoffberg, Judith A. *Artwords and Bookworks: An International Exhibition of
   Recent Artists' Books and Ephemera : Los Angeles Institute of Contemporary
   Art, 28 February–30 March 1978.* Los Angeles: LAICA, 1978.
Hompson, Davi Det, ed. *An International Encyclopedia of Plans and
   Occurrences.* Richmond, VA: Virginia Commonwealth University, 1973.
Isgrò, Emilio. *Proletarismo e dittatura della poesia. Guendalina Fraser Valerio.*
   Milano: Studio Santandrea, 1971.
Kostelanetz, Richard, ed. *Language and Structure in North America.* Toronto:
   Kensington Arts Association, 1975.
Lepage, Jacques, ed. *Hors Langage.* Nice: Théâtre de Nice, 1973.
———, ed. *Poésie de recherche.* Nice: 1968
Lora-Totino, Arrigo, Adriano Spatola, and Franco Verdi, eds. *Esposizione
   internazionale di poesia sperimentale.* Casterlfranco, Italy: 1967.
Mahlow, Dietrich, ed. *Schrift und bild.* Amsterdam: Stedelijk Museum, 1963.
Menna, Filiberto, Italo Mussa, and Lamberto Pignotti, eds. *La scrittura.*
   Rome: Galleria Seconda Scala, 1976.
Palazzoli, Daniela, ed. *I denti del drago.* Milan: Galleria l'uomo e l'arte
   Milano, 1972.
Parmiggiani, Claudio and Adriano Spatola, eds. *Parole Sui Muri. (Fiumalbo
   1967).* Torino: Geiger, 1968.
Perfetti, Michele, ed. *Comunicazioni Visive.* Massafra, Italy, 1968.
———, ed. *Rassegna nazionale di poesia visiva.* Taranto: 1968.

Plaza, Julio and Walter Zanini, eds. *Prospectiva 74*. São Paulo: Museu de Arte Contemporanea, 1974.

Poesia experimental. Barcelona: Istituto aleman – Colegio de arquitectos, 1973.

Reichardt, Jasia, ed. *Between Poetry and Painting*. London: Institute of Contemporary Arts, 1965.

Rook, Gerrit Jan de. Anthologie visuele poëzie = Visual poetry anthology : supplement. Utrecht: 't Hoogt, 1975. As a complement to this catalog, see the same author's *Historische anthologie visuele poëzie* (Brussel: Rijkscentrum Hoger Kunstonderwijs, 1976).

Spatola, Adriano, and Franco Verdi. *Esposizione internazionale di poesia sperimentale: Modena, Galleria della sala di cultura, 1–12 giugno 1966*. Modena: La Galleria, 1966.

Spatola, Adriano, ed. *La forma della scrittura*. Bologna: Galleria Comunale d'Arte Moderna, 1977.

Verdi, Franco, ed. *Segni nello spazio: Catalogo edito dall'Azienda autonomo di soggiorno Trieste per l'espozione Internazionale "Segni nello spazio", Castello di San Giusto, 8/31 luglio 1967*. Verona: Litografia Cortella, 1967.

Vree, Paul de, Reinhard Döhl, and Bob Cobbing. *Klankteksten, konkrete poëzie, visuele teksten = Sound texts, concrete poetry, visual texts = Akustische Texte, konkrete Poesie, visuelle Texte*. Catalogus, nr. 492. Amsterdam: Stedelijk Museum, 1971.

Weiermair, Peter, and Siegfried J. Schmidt. *Visuelle Poesie = Visual poetry = Poesia visuale = Poésie visuelle*. Wien: Österreichisches College, 1968.

CRITICAL REFERENCES

Accame, Vincenzo. *Il segno poetico, riferimenti per una storia della ricerca poetico-visuale e interdisciplinare*. Samedan, Svizzera: Munt, 1977.

———. "Poesia sperimentale ed esperimenti di poesia." *Bollettino Tool* 1 (1968).

Altmann, Roberto. "Le lettrisme poétique." *Linea sud* 5/6 (1967).

Anceschi, Giovanni. "Intorno alla Estetica di Bense." *M. Bense, Estetica*. Ed. Giovanni Anceschi. Milan: Bompiani, 1974. Particularly the paragraph "Bense e la letteratura."

Balestrini, Nanni. "Poesia visiva." *Linea sud* 2 (1965).

Ballerini, Luigi. *La piramide capovolta*. Venice: Editor Marsilio, 1975.

Bartoli, Francesco. "Scrittura visuale." *Letteratura*. Ed. Gabriele Scaramazza. Milan: Enciclopedia Feltrinelli Fischer, 1976.

Belloli, Carlo. "La componente visuale-tipografica nella poesia d'avanguardia." *Pagina* 3 (1963).

———. "Corpi di poesia; poesia visuale; testo-poema." *Il compasso* 1 (1966).

———. *Poesia concreta e musica elettronica*. Bergamo: Studio 2B, 1967.

Bense, Max. "Stili sperimentali." *Modulo* 1 (1966).

———. *Teoria testuale della poesia.* Rome: Silva, 1969.

Bonito-Oliva, Achille. "Poesia visiva." *Presenza sud, n.* 1, 1968.

Campos, Haroldo de. "Poesia concreta brasiliana." *Malebolge* 1 (1967).

Campos, Augusto de, Décio Pignatari, and Haroldo de Campos. *Teoria da poesia concreta; textos críticos e manifestos, 1950–1960.* São Paulo: Edições Invenção, 1965.

Carrega, Ugo. "Cronistoria della poesia grafica in Italia." *Il bimestre* 18/19 (1972).

Castro, Ernesto Manuel de Melo e. *A proposição 2.01: textos [sobre] poesia experimental, seguidos de uma compilação breve de poemas experimentais e de bibliografias para informação do leitor.* Lisbon: Edizioni Ulisseia, 1965.

Chopin, Henri. "Introduction à la poésie du son." *Vers univers* 1 (1966).

Curi, Fausto. "La distruzione del modello lineare e la letteratura d'avanguardia." *Metodo storia strutture,* Paravia, 1971.

D'Ambrosio, Matteo. "Dalla poesia collage alla poesia visiva." *Annali della facolta di lettere a filosofia dell'universita di Napoli* XVI.4 (1974).

———. *Bibliografia della poesia italiana d'avanguardia (visiva, visuale, concreta e fonetica).* Rome: Bulzoni, 1977.

De Alexandris, Sandro. "Ricerca sperimentale e grafica pubblicitaria." *Linea grafica* 5 (1966).

Döhl, Reinhard and Eugen Gomringer. *Poesía experimental: estudios y teoría.* Madrid: Instituto Alemán de Madrid, 1967.

Dorfles, Gillo. "Poesia concreta (poesia visuale, poesia trovata, poesia tecnologica, poesia sperimentale)." *Modulo* 1 (1966).

———. "Rapporti e interference tra le arti oggi," *La battana* 18 (1969).

Favari, Pietro. "Strumenti verbali e iconici nella scrittura poetica italiana." *D'ars* 70 (1974).

Gappmayr, Heinz. "La poesia del concreto." *Modulo* 1 (1966).

———. "Sinossi delle caratteristiche della poesia tradizionale o visuale." *Bollettino Tool* 1 (1968).

Garnier, Pierre. *Spatialisme et poésie concrète.* Paris: Editions Gallimard, 1968.

Giuliani, Alfredo. "Scheda personale sulla voce 'collage'." *Linea sud* 2 (1965).

Gomringer, Eugen. "Dal verso alla costellazione, scopo e forma di una nuova poesia." *Modulo* 1 (1966).

Higgins, Dick. *Foewꝗombwhnw.* New York: Something Else Press, 1969.

Hausmann, Raoul. "Introduction à une histoire du poème phonétique." *Les lettres* 34 (1965).

Heissenbüttel, Helmut. "Per una storia della poesia visiva nel ventesimo secolo." *Il verri* 16 (1964).

Houédard, Dom Sylvester. *Between poetry and painting: chronology*, attached to a catologue from an anonymous exhibition.

———. "Concrete poetry – Ian Hamilton Finlay." *Typographica* 8 (1963).

Lora-Totino, Arrigo. "Poesia sperimentale e ricerca grafica." *Linea grafica* 5 (1966).

———. "Ragioni di una scelta per un'antologia della poesia concreta." *Modulo* 1 (1966).

———. Text in the pamphlet *Poesia concreta e musica elettronica*. Bergamo: Studio 2B, 1967.

———. "Dalla cosa pubblica delle lettere al laboratorio della lingua." *Arte e poesia* 11/14 (1971).

Machiedo, Mladen. *Orientamenti ideologico-estetici nella poesia italiana del dopoguerra*. Zagreb: Filozofski Fakultet, 1973.

Marcucci, Lucia. "Il diritto di essere poeti." *La battana* 18 (1969).

Marinetti, Filippo Tommaso, and Luciano De Maria. *Teoria e invenzione futurista*. Milano: A. Mondadori, 1968.

Miccini, Eugenio. "Poesia visiva." *Linea sud* 2 (1965).

Moles, Abraham. "Manifesto dell'arte permutazionale." *Malebolge* 1 (1967).

Mon, Franz. "Textes dans l'espace." *Les lettres* 31 (1963).

Marrocchi, Giuseppe. "Poesia visiva." *Comunicazioni di massa*. Ed. Pio Balzelli. Milan: Enciclopedia Feltrinelli Fischer, 1974.

Munari, Carlo. "Il surrealismo e la pubblicità." *Siprauno* 6 (1964).

Nanni, Luciano. "Lo sperimentalismo poetico novecentesco e la crisi dell'aesthetica borghese." *Estetica e societa tecnologica*, Il Mulino, 1976.

Nazzaro, G. B. "Le parole in liberta." *Introduzione al futurismo*. Naples: Guida, 1973.

Padín, Clemente. *De la représentation à l'action: [les anartistes]*. Marseilles: Nouvelles éditions polaires, 1975.

Pétronio, Arthur. "Verbophonie et poème-fiction." *Vers univers* 3 (1966).

Pignotti, Lamberto. *Istruzioni per l'uso degli ultimi modelli di poesia*. Rome: Lerici, 1968.

Popper, Frank. "Notes sur la poésie cinétique." *Approches* 1 (1966).

Porta, Antonio. "Poesia visiva." *Linea sud* 2 (1965).

Schwitters, Kurt. "Consistent Poetry." *Poems, Performance Pieces, Proses, Plays, Poetics*. Ed. Jerome Rothenberg and Pierre Joris. Philadelphia: Temple University Press, 1993. 223–225.

Šmejkal, František. "Gli oggetti di Jiří Kolár." *Terzo occhio* 3 (1975).

Sitta, C.A. "La poesia elementare, 6 domande a Luciano Anceschi." *Tam Tam* 10/11/12 (1975).

Weaver, Mike. "Concrete poetry." *The Lugano Review* 5/6 (1966).

Tzara, Tristan. *Seven Dada manifestos and Lampisteries.* London: Calder, 1977.

Zagoričnik, Franci. *Navodilo za uporabo; Istruzioni per l'uso.* Ljubljana, Yugoslavia: Edicija Gong, 1975.

Visualizing A Total Poetics:
Adriano Spatola's Verso la poesia totale

Guy Bennett

> *Every poetics claims to be the only poetics, but poetics are infinite in number.*
>
> — LUCIANO ANCESCHI

Toward Total Poetry is a pivotal book in the history of avant-garde poetics, oscillating as it does between three distinct moments: written in the late 1960s and revised a decade later, it documents the experimental poetries of that time, considers their relationship and debt to the avant-garde poetries of the early twentieth century, and suggests their potential evolution into a "total poetry" of the future. It is also pivotal in an epistemological sense, since it sits (uncomfortably, I might add) between modernism and postmodernism. Even in its rhetorical strategy the book pivots between opposite poles, as it is both atomizing and totalizing in the presentation of its subject matter, and phenomenological and visionary in its analysis.

The latter two oppositional pairs are perhaps the most striking features of the notion of "total poetry," which Spatola defines as an attempt to "establish the need to see the field of experimental poetry not so much as a confused, fragmentary area in dispersion, but as the coexistence of various lines of march bound up in a dense network of connections and exchanges." (p. 20) The "various lines of march" in question here include concrete poetry, visual poetry, sound poetry, kinetic poetry, collage poetry, painting poetry, etc., in a word, the entire range of experimental poetic writing conceived not as so many different types of poetry or approaches to poetic creation, but as different facets of a single, total poetry. Spatola further hoped that in its evolution, poetry would eventually avail itself of all forms of cultural production, and thus fuse into a single, total medium:

> The problem is not only to transform poetry into something new compared to poetic tradition, but above all that through this transformation poetry become a total art. New experimental poetry is no longer exclusively interpretable as a force modifying the usual instruments of poetic creation, or as the necessity of overcoming national linguistic barriers to an explicitly international poetry: today it seeks to become a total medium, to escape all limitations, to include theater, photography, music, painting, typography, cinematographic techniques, and every other aspect of culture, in a utopian ambition to return to origins. (p. 22)

Set out in these terms, Spatola's "total poetry" strongly recalls the Wagnerian notion of the *Gesamtkunstwerk* or "total work of art." This of course was Wagner's conception of opera, which brings together music, poetry, acting, as well as elements of architecture, sculpture, and painting. Though the end product is different (for Wagner, it is a question of musical drama; for Spatola a dramatic reconceptualization of experimental writing, ontologically speaking), in both cases the underlying idea is the same: various artforms and media combine to create a new "total media," the whole of which is greater than the sum of its parts.

It is interesting to note that the temporal oscillation evoked above comes into play in both of these concepts; both total poetry and the total work of art are presented as the future products of a utopian vision based on the idea of a return to an earlier, idealized state. Whereas Wagner speaks of a return to antiquity, when classical tragedy incorporated an ideal combination of music, poetry, and dance, Spatola refers to a "return to origins" presumably of writing, whose initial pictographic, ideographic, and phonogrammatic roots, as well as its graphic and gestural qualities, are reflected in the experimental writings that he championed.

There is a shared socio-political dimension to these concepts as well: as Barry Millington has written, "the reuniting of constituent parts in the *Gesamtkunstwerk* mirrored the socialist aim of restoring integrity to a fragmented, divided society."* For Spatola, on the other hand, the hope was that total poetry would bring about a reintegration of art (specifically, language art) into public life and discourse, which were seen as increasingly dominated by mass communication technologies. "The task of the new poetry," he writes, "seems to be that of rendering sociologically active a linguistic reality that risks remaining 'private,' and without contact with the world." (p. 22)

The contact could also be established by involving the reader more deeply in the work during the reading process. The argument goes something like this: the more "open" a text, the more active the reader must become to negotiate it, adopting the role of participant, collaborator, and ultimately co-author of the work:

> The totalizing gesture of the new poetry is always, somehow, an attempt to involve the reader on all levels, to make him an accomplice today, and a co-author tomorrow: according to [Mary Ellen] Solt, the reader "must now perceive the poem as an object and participate in the poet's act of creating it." (p. 40–41)

Let's not forget that *Toward Total Poetry* was a product of the same era as Umberto Eco's *Open Work,* and Roland Barthes' "The Death of the Author" and "From Work to Text," all of which declared that the reader had become central – one could (and perhaps should) say instrumental – to the "completion" of the work. The above statement, in which the reader is described as a participant in the text's creation, is reminiscent of Eco's statement that "'Open' works are brought to a conclusion by the performer at the very moment he experiences them aesthetically,"† and of Barthes' no less explicit claim that "The Text requires that one try to abolish (or at the very least to diminish) the distance between writing and reading, in no

---

* "Gesamtkunstwerk," *New Grove Guide to Wagner and His Operas* (Cary, NC: Oxford University Press, 2006) 151.

† *Opera aperta* (Milano: Bompiani, 1962) 33. My translation.

way by intensifying the projection of the reader into the work but by joining them in a single signifying practice."*

The emphasis placed on an interactive, performative reading process described here is also characteristic of electronic hypertext and hypermedia literature, as by their very nature the latter do demand an active involvement on the part of the reader who becomes a de facto collaborator (within the parameters defined by the author, of course) of that instance of the work generated by his own reading of it. In fact, in the case of much electronic literature, we could say that there is no text per se, but rather a potential or latent literary work that only comes into being when the reader reads/performs/plays it. Such work is not so very different from the print-based visual and sound poetry championed by Spatola, which likewise needs a reader to actuate it; indeed it may be the closest we have ever come to a total-media total poetry as described above, since these works do typically involve text, sound, still and moving imagery, etc.

The poetics of the whole invoked by Spatola in *Toward Total Poetry* is neither the first nor the last instance of a practicing poet or artist proposing a totalizing metadiscourse intended to circumscribe the entire field of activity within which he is operating. I would like to mention two other examples here. The first is El Lissitzky and Hans Arp's *The Isms of Art* of 1925. This primarily visual history of the avant-garde from 1914–1924 comprises photographic presentations of and textual commentary on a variety of modernist movements, including many of the usual suspects – Futurism, Dada, Expressionism, et al – as well as of some movements and concepts today largely forgotten, such as Compressionism and Metaphysicism. The fact that the latter either morphed into something else or disappeared from the page of history altogether demonstrates one of the major challenges to constructing totalizing systems: the territories they seek to chart are not fixed but evolving, and the boundaries that demarcate them are constantly shifting to contain the new reality. By the time the system has been

---

* "From Work to Text," *Image – Music – Text*, Trans. Stephen Heath (New York: Hill and Wang, 1977) 162.

put in place, it no longer corresponds to the total area it purports to document.

A more recent example of a "total poetics" is Jerome and Diane Rothenberg's 1987 *Symposium of The Whole*. This historical anthology, subtitled "A Range of Discourse Toward an Ethnopoetics," includes texts on various ancient and "primitive" mythopoeic practices and their connections to and influences on contemporary writing, and presents as a whole a broad and disparate array of ethnopoetries. However expansive its vision, it is tempered by the cautionary "toward" in the subtitle: as in *Toward Total Poetry,* it suggests that a totality has been conceived of but has yet to be achieved. This potentiality is in fact inherent in "poetics of the whole" generally speaking: they can only ever be poetics of becoming. As mentioned above, we never achieve a fixed, immutable whole since their object of study is always inevitably "in process."

Though it may seem like splitting hairs, it is also interesting to consider the use of the indefinite article in the subtitle of *Symposium of The Whole*: "Toward an Ethnopoetics," as opposed to that of the definite article in Spatola's *Verso la poesia totale*. That definite article posed a problem for the translation of the title, which in the end we rendered as *Toward Total Poetry,* though a more "natural" feeling English version would be "Toward a Total Poetry," i.e. with the indefinite article, as in the Rothenberg book. The use of the definite article in Italian, like the elimination of the indefinite article in the English, suggests that this future poetry is more, well, definite, and this momentary flash of certainty gives a glimpse of the modernist ethos that permeates the book, in spite of its ultimately postmodern vision.

Toward Total Poetry sits on the cusp of these two conflicting paradigms, one dominated by the belief in a definable, delimitable, rationally ordered totality, the other by a tendency toward plurality, hybridity, and a suspicion of totalizing systems. Poetics may be infinite in number, to quote Anceschi once again, but each one proposes to be the only one. In embracing the infinite and the one, *Toward Total Poetry* would like to be both.

Index of Names

Other titles from Otis Books / Seismicity Editions

J. Reuben Appelman, *Make Loneliness*
Published 2008 | 84 pages | $12.95
ISBN-10: 0-9796177-0-7
ISBN-13: 978-0-9796177-0-6

Guy Bennett and Béatrice Mousli, Editors, *Seeing Los Angeles:
A Different Look at a Different City*
Published 2007 | 202 pages | $12.95
ISBN-10: 0-9755924-9-1
ISBN-13: 978-0-9755924-9-6

Jean-Michel Espitallier, *Espitallier's Theorem*
Translated from the French by Guy Bennett
Published 2003 | 137 pages | $12.95
ISBN: 0-9755924-2-4

Norman M. Klein, *Freud in Coney Island and Other Tales*
Published 2006 | 104 pages | $12.95
ISBN: 0-9755924-6-7

Ken McCullough, *Left Hand*
Published 2004 | 191 pages | $12.95
ISBN: 0-9755924-1-6

Béatrice Mousli, Editor, *Review of Two Worlds:
French and American Poetry in Translation*
Published 2005 | 148 pages | $12.95
ISBN: 0-9755924-3-2

Ryan Murphy, *Down with the Ship*
Published 2006 | 66 pages | $12.95
ISBN: 0-9755924-5-9

Hélène Sanguinetti, *Hence This Cradle*
Translated from the French by Ann Cefola
Published 2007 | 160 pages | $12.95
ISBN: 970-0-9755924-7-2

Janet Sarbanes, *Army of One*
Published 2008 | 173 pages | $12.95
ISBN-10: 0-9796177-1-5
ISBN-13: 978-0-9796177-1-3

Severo Sarduy, *Beach Birds*
    Translated from the Spanish by Suzanne Jill Levine and Carol Maier
    Published 2007 | 182 pages | $12.95
    ISBN: 978-9755924-8-9

Carol Treadwell, *Spots and Trouble Spots*
    Published 2004 | 176 pages | $12.95
    ISBN: 0-9755924-0-8

Allyssa Wolf, *Vaudeville*
    Published 2006 | 82 pages | $12.95
    ISBN: 0-9755924-4

Forthcoming in 2009

Bruce Bégout, *Common Place. The American Motel.*
    Translated from the French by Colin Keaveney

Eric Priestley, *For Keeps.*

Sophie Rachmul, *Los Angeles 1950–1990 – The Emergence of an Artistic Scene
    and of a Poetic Discourse on the City.*
    Translated from the French by Mindy Menjou